Participation of the Poor in Development Initiatives

For Eric

Participation of the Poor in Development Initiatives

Taking Their Rightful Place

Carolyn M Long

Institute for
Development
Research

IDR

Earthscan Publications Ltd, London and Sterling, VA

First published in the UK and USA in 2001 by
Earthscan Publications Ltd

Copyright © Institute for Development Research, 2001

ISBN: 1 85383 761 X paperback
       1 85383 760 1 hardback

Typesetting by PCS Mapping & DTP, Newcastle upon Tyne
Printed and bound by
Creative Print & Design Wales (Ebbw Vale)
Index prepared by Indexing Specialists, Hove, East Sussex, www.indexing.co.uk

For a full list of publications please contact:
Earthscan Publications Ltd
120 Pentonville Road
London, N1 9JN, UK
Tel: +44 (0)20 7278 0433
Fax: +44 (0)20 7278 1142
Email: earthinfo@earthscan.co.uk
http://www.earthscan.co.uk

22883 Quicksilver Drive, Sterling, VA 20166–2012, USA

A catalogue record for this book is available from the British Library

Library of Congress Cataloging-in-Publication Data

Long, Carolyn.
Participation of the poor in development initiatives : taking their rightful place /
Carolyn Long.
    p. cm.
  Includes bibliographical references and index.
  ISBN 1–85383–760–1 (cloth) — ISBN 1–85383–761–X (pbk.)
   1. Poor—Developing countries. 2. Economic assistance—Developing countries.
   3. Economic development projects—Developing countries. 4. Nonprofit
   organizations—Developing countries. I. Title.

HC59.72.P6 L66 2001
338.9'009172'4—dc21

                                                                    2001023291

Earthscan is an editorially independent subsidiary of Kogan Page Ltd and publishes
in association with WWF-UK and the International Institute for Environment and
Development

This book is printed on elemental chlorine-free paper

Contents

Tables, Figures and Boxes

TABLES

FIGURES

BOXES

Acknowledgements

In November 1998, the conference entitled *Upscaling and Mainstreaming Participation of Primary Stakeholders: Lessons Learned and Ways Forward* was held at World Bank headquarters in Washington, DC. The NGO Working Group on the World Bank conceived the idea for the conference and enrolled as co-sponsors the World Bank, the Swedish International Development Cooperation Authority (Sida), the US Agency for International Development (USAID), German Technical Cooperation (Gesellschaft für Technische Zusammearbeit) (GTZ), the Department for International Development (DFID), and the Institute for Development Studies (IDS). The conference served as the impetus for this book, which was commissioned by the NGO Working Group on the World Bank. The book draws extensively on the proceedings of those two days and also takes a retrospective look at more than a decade of work by donors, non-governmental organization (NGO) activists and others to incorporate participation of the poor into donor agencies.

Thanks go to the co-sponsors of the conference for their commitments of time, resources and willingness to publicly examine the record of donor agencies in involving poor and marginalized people in their programmes. Thanks are also due to NGOs around the world who have promoted participation of the poor over many years and in particular, the members, past and present, of the NGO Working Group on the World Bank for their advocacy of participation at the World Bank for more than a decade. The NGOs who monitored and wrote case studies of participation in World Bank projects and policy processes made an important contribution to our understanding of the challenges of incorporating participation into donor processes. A special debt of gratitude goes to Rajesh Tandon, who served as chairperson of the NGO Working Group on the World Bank's Sub-Committee on Participation from 1994 to 1998, and to Manuel Chiriboga, chairperson of the NGO Working Group on the World

Bank during those years. Together, they led the NGO Working Group on the World Bank's efforts on participation during five years and saw this book as a way to continue to assist activists – in NGOs, inside donor agencies, academic and research institutes, and recipient government agencies – who are working towards complete mainstreaming of participation in donor initiatives.

The full manuscript was reviewed by L David Brown, Manuel Chiriboga, Jane Covey, John Gaventa, Rajesh Tandon, Warren Van Wicklin and Aubrey Williams. I am grateful as well for many insights gained from conversations with David, Manuel, Jane and Rajesh. Olivier Carduner and Brian Pratt reviewed Chapters 1 and 4, and 1 and 3, respectively. Chapter 4 also benefitted from a thoughtful review by Elise Storck.

The Institute for Development Research (IDR) has provided organizational, logistical and moral support throughout this project. Jane Covey, its president, has been an invaluable source of support, encouragement and inspiration throughout the entire process. Hope Steele prepared the manuscript for publication; Deborah Grose organized the references, and Archana Kalegaonkar, formerly with IDR, provided support earlier on in the process.

Sheila Mahony provided research assistance, tracking down information, and ferreting out dates and sources. Thanks are also due to the many people in NGOs and donor agencies who provided information, interpreted events and helped to tell the story as fully as possible. Many thanks also to my dear friend, Patricia Aburdene, a best-selling author, for her support and advice on writing the book.

My husband, Scott Brumburgh, has been unfailingly patient and supportive, as well as substantively helpful on a variety of issues related to organizational change. I am very grateful to him, as well as to our son, Eric, whose patience, love and pride in his mother's work have been inspiring!

Last, I want to express my profound respect and admiration to the people all over the world striving to take their rightful place and to those who assist them in doing so. It is a privilege and honour to work in international development and to witness the power of the human spirit at work in efforts towards just and sustainable development.

Acronyms and Abbreviations

ACVFA	Advisory Committee on Voluntary Foreign Aid
ADS	Automated Directives System
AGEREF	Association de la Gestion des Ressources de la Faune (associations of primary stakeholders)
AVARD	Association of Voluntary Agencies for Rural Development
the Board	the World Bank's Board
BIC	Bank Information Center
BMZ	German Ministry of Economic Cooperation and Development
BRAC	Bangladesh Rural Advancement Committee
CAS	Country Assistance Strategy
CDF	Comprehensive Development Framework
CDIE	Center for Development Information and Evaluation
CIDA	Canadian International Development Agency
CIDP-I	First Rural Communal Irrigation Development Project
CIDP-II	Second Rural Communal Irrigation Development Project
CSO	Civil Society Organization
D'GAP	The Development Group for Alternative Policies
DAC	Development Assistance Committee
DFID	Department for International Development
DPEP II	District Primary Education Project
EDI	Economic Development Institute (of the World Bank)
EDUCO	Educación con Participación de la Communidad
ESW	economic and sector work
EU	European Union
FAO	Food and Agricultural Organization (of the United Nations)
FAVDO	Forum of African Voluntary Development Organizations

FIAHS	Fund for Innovative Approaches in Human and Social Development
GEPRENAF	Gestion Participative des Ressources Naturelles et de la Faune (Community-based Natural Resource and Wildlife Management Project)
GPRA	Government Performance Results Act
GTZ	Gesellschaft für Technische Zusammenarbeit (German Technical Cooperation)
IBRD	International Bank for Reconstruction and Development
IDA	International Development Association
IDB	Inter-American Development Bank
IDR	Institute for Development Research
IDS	Institute for Development Studies (University of Sussex)
IIED	International Institute for Environment and Development
IFAD	International Fund for Agricultural Development
IGP	Inter-Agency Group on Participation
IMF	International Monetary Fund
INADES	Institut Africain pour le Développement Economique et Social – Centre Africain de Formation
INTRAC	International NGO Training and Research Centre
LAMP	Learning and Action to Mainstream Participation
Learning group	Learning Group on Popular Participation at the World Bank
NGO	non-governmental organization
NGOWG	NGO Working Group on the World Bank
NIA	National Irrigation Administration
ODA	Overseas Development Authority
OED	Operations Evaluation Department (of the World Bank)
OECD/DAC	Organization for Economic Cooperation and Development/Development Assistance Committee
ORAP	Organization of Rural Associations for Progress
Oxfam GB	Oxfam Great Britain
Oxfam UK and Ireland	Oxfam United Kingdom and Ireland
PAL	Participatory Action Learning Program
pers com	personal communication
PRIA	Society for Participatory Research in Asia
PROINDER	Proyecto de Alivio a la Probreza e Iniciativas Rurales
Results Act	(US) Government Performance Results Act
RADI	Réseau Africain pour le Développement Intègre
SAPRI	Structural Adjustment Participatory Review Initiative

SAPRIN	Structural Adjustment Participatory Review Initiative Network
SARAR	Self-esteem, Associative strength, Resourcefulness, Action planning and Responsibility
SEHAS	Servicio Habitaciónal y de Acción Social
Sida	Swedish International Development Cooperation Authority
SWCB	Soil and Water Conservation Branch
UK	United Kingdom
UNDP	United Nations Development Programme
US	United States
USAID	United States Agency for International Development
WDR–2000	World Development Report 2000
WEOB	Women's Eyes on the [World] Bank
Working Group	NGO Working Group on the World Bank (NGOWG)
ZOPP	Zielorientierte Projektplanung

Foreword

As an integral part of the practice of social mobilization at the grass-roots level, participatory development was already the common language among NGOs in different parts of the world by the early 1970s. However, national governments and international agencies continued to believe in top-down, externally designed development programmes, despite mounting evidence of their inefficiency and unsustainability. Many NGO colleagues and networks at the national and global levels had begun to point out the need for an alternative bottom-up, participatory development model.

At the onset of the 1990s, the NGO Working Group on the World Bank decided to advocate the need for this approach with the World Bank in its own projects and policies. It brought together, under Southern leadership, NGO representatives from both developing and developed countries to question the World Bank regarding its policies, programmes and loans. In the 1990s it focused its main advocacy efforts on two issues: structural adjustment programmes and primary stakeholder participation (participation of the poor and marginalized).

This book reflects the outcome of the interventions of the Working Group on the World Bank's policies and procedures in relation to participation and participatory development over this decade. Many activists argued that global institutions such as the World Bank are so large, complex and powerful that attempts to change them can be exercises in futility. Our colleagues in our own institutions as well as within the NGO community had similar reservations when we used our resources and efforts to attempt to influence the World Bank on promoting and supporting participatory development in its projects and policies throughout the world.

We believe that our efforts were worthwhile, and significant progress has been made although we cannot see it as a finished effort: advocacy for meaningful participation has to continue. We also feel that the NGO Working Group on the World Bank was able to focus its attention on the participation of primary stakeholders, for whose benefits such projects are intended and who are likely to be affected by such projects. This emphasis on the participation of the poor and the excluded (including women and indigenous people) was a unique thrust of the effort launched by the NGO Working Group on the World Bank: it also convened a broad-based multi-stakeholder conference in Washington, DC, in November 1998. The conference was able to review the progress made, not only in the World Bank, but also in bilateral agencies, including USAID, GTZ, DFID and Sida.

Another significant milestone of this effort has been raising the issue of primary stakeholder participation in policy formulation. This is indeed a more complex and ambiguous arena, requiring experimentation and exploration. But we believe that unless the poor are involved in thinking about policy (related to macro-economic and sector policies, education, health, drinking water, forestry, and agricultural development for example), policy formulation will be determined by distant experts, thereby reducing the ownership and appropriateness of such policies.

This volume, therefore, attempts to bring together the lessons learnt regarding advocacy on issues concerning promoting, sustaining and supporting primary stakeholder participation in developing projects and policies of multilateral and bilateral development organizations. We hope that such lessons can be useful to future advocacy endeavours, as the struggle for participation is a fundamental part of having real participation happen.

We are grateful to our colleagues in the NGO Working Group on the World Bank, who brought their rich experience and helped monitor World Bank policies and projects; to our collaborating partners and institutions, committed colleagues at the World Bank and other agencies who have stood with us, in support and in challenge, throughout this process from 1994 to 1998, when we were chairpersons of the NGO Working Group on the World Bank and its sub-committee on participation, respectively.

We appreciate the effort put in by Carolyn Long, a long-time NGO colleague and advocate for World Bank reform, in preparing this manuscript, and are grateful to IDR for its support.

Manuel Chiriboga,
Asociacion Latinoamericana de Organizaciones de Promocion
(ALOP), San Jose, Costa Rica

Rajesh Tandon,
Society for Participatory Research in Asia (PRIA),
New Delhi, India

April 2001

Chapter 1

Introduction

In February 1990, in a small town outside Johannesburg, South Africa, Nelson Mandela walked out of prison a free man after 27 years to begin his march towards the presidency of his country four years later. As the world knows, his election put an end to legal apartheid. Mandela's freedom and his eventual election were the culmination of years of effort by ordinary South Africans struggling for freedom and supported by people all over the world. On that same day, about 3000 miles to the northeast, at Arusha in Tanzania, an international conference on popular participation was taking place. This conference had been planned jointly by non-governmental organizations (NGOs) from Africa, Europe, Canada and the United States, together with the United Nations Economic Commission for Africa. Its purpose was to call attention to the essential truth that people must be integrally involved in their own development. That conference, occurring in perfect symmetry with the liberation of Nelson Mandela, produced the *African Charter on Popular Participation*, which stands to this day as perhaps the best expression of popular participation (African Charter, 1990).

At the same time that the Arusha conference was taking place, in other parts of the world an increasing number of multilateral and bilateral donor agencies were undertaking efforts to adopt participatory practices in their own operations. Many development practitioners trace initial donor interest in participation to the *World Conference on Agricultural and Rural Development* in 1979 led by the United Nations Food and Agricultural Organization (FAO) (Pratt, 2000). Subsequently, many other donors followed suit. Five of these donors and their work on participation are the subject of this book. They include the World Bank, the Swedish International Development Cooperation Authority (Sida), Gesellschaft für Technische

Zusammenarbeit/German Technical Cooperation (GTZ), the United States Agency for International Development (USAID) and the Department for International Development (DFID) (formerly known as the Overseas Development Authority or ODA). The convergence of interest of these international donor agencies in participation in the late 1980s and early 1990s signified a major shift in development thinking.

This book will look back at the results achieved by these international donor agencies in adopting participatory practices and in making the organizational and policy changes necessary to encourage and facilitate such practice; and at the results NGOs have had as advocates in promoting participation of the poor in large donor agencies' programmes. It will focus on participation of the poor in large donor agencies' projects and development policy formulation. *Primary stakeholders* are poor and marginalized people expected to benefit from donor-funded projects or policies. *Primary stakeholder participation* is defined as involvement of poor and marginalized people in decision-making roles regarding all important aspects of donor-funded projects or policies.

This chapter presents the historical background and evolutionary thinking leading to present-day understanding of participation, as well as a framework of terms and definitions.

BACKGROUND

For more than 20 years, the participation of poor and marginalized people in development initiatives intended to benefit them has been acknowledged as important in achieving sustainable development. Why? Because who better than poor people themselves can understand their economic and social conditions and the problems they face, and have insights that can help shape initiatives intended to benefit them? Such participation was not a regular part of project design and implementation for the first 30 years of development efforts – and still is not a routine part of project design today. In 1981, Sida was among the first donor institutions to launch formal efforts to engage the poor and marginalized through its Strategy for Rural Development. Popular participation was viewed as an objective in itself – that is, a basic democratic right that should be promoted in all development projects (Rudqvist, 1992). In 1986, GTZ named the participation of the poor as one of five quality criteria to be used in its work (Forster, 1998). The World Bank followed suit in 1990 by creating a Learning Group on Popular Participation (referred to as the Learning Group) to study and understand participation with a view to incorporating what it learned into its operations. In 1993, USAID launched a complete reform process of the agency to re-orient itself towards its 'customers' (the poor) and hold itself accountable for results that its customers value (LaVoy and Charles, 1998). USAID had worked to incorporate participation in its projects for many years prior to this, but the 1993 reform represented a new level of commitment to the poor. Lastly, DFID became concerned with participatory approaches to development in the early 1990s, and in 1995 outlined guidance for operational staff in its *Technical Note on Stakeholder Participation in Development Projects* (Norton, 1998).

These efforts at understanding and incorporating participation of the poor into donor operations have benefited from – and in many ways, been accelerated by – advocacy and monitoring efforts carried out by NGOs around the world. For bilateral agencies, much of the advocacy has been carried out by national NGOs in the country of the donor, and sometimes by Southern NGOs who are recipients of such aid. As for the World Bank, NGOs around the world have involved themselves in advocacy and monitoring of its participation efforts. The most consistent, long-term NGO voice advocating participation at the World Bank has been the NGO Working Group on the World Bank, henceforth referred to as 'the Working Group'. In 1981, the World Bank created the NGO–World Bank Committee to facilitate dialogue and collaboration. By 1984, NGO members of the committee had established the Working Group as an autonomous parallel body that included only NGOs. The Working Group advocates World Bank reform and does so through policy dialogue with it: it establishes its own *advocacy* priorities, its agenda for meetings with the World Bank, and its operating policies and procedures. The joint NGO–World Bank Committee is the forum for dialogue between World Bank staff and the Working Group (Covey, 1998).

It must be noted that there were many forces promoting participation in donor agencies in addition to NGOs and those inside the organizations themselves. For example, from the late 1980s onwards workshops held at the Institute for Development Studies (IDS), many of them jointly with the International Institute for Environment and Development (IIED), brought together experience with participation.[1] Much of this derived from participatory rural appraisal. In the early 1990s, participatory rural appraisal spread rapidly through training, networking, South–South exchanges and publications, and was soon being required for projects by many donor agencies.

Robert Chambers of the IDS was asked by World Bank staff to provide workshops on incentives and rewards which would promote participation. IDS is a leader in the study and promotion of participation in development.

In order to review the record of effort by these donors to incorporate participation of the poor into development operations, the Working Group proposed a multi-stakeholder conference, which was held in November 1998 at the World Bank's headquarters in Washington, DC. Entitled *Upscaling and Mainstreaming Participation of Primary Stakeholders: Lessons Learned and Ways Forward*, this Participation Conference provided a stocktaking of the experiences of the past 15 years, delineated the lessons learned from this work, and charted the way forward. Conceived and promoted by the Working Group, the conference was co-sponsored by the World Bank, Sida, GTZ, DFID, USAID, IDS and the Working Group itself. These co-sponsors jointly planned the conference. Donors made presentations there about their experiences in participatory project development and policy formulation, and about efforts to reform their organizations to incorporate participation of the poor in their operations. The Working Group presented results from monitoring World Bank-funded projects and policy formulation processes. Conference participants included representatives of multilateral and bilateral donors, foundations, recipient governments, Southern and Northern NGOs and academics.

The three themes of the Participation Conference were:

1   the results for projects, policy development processes and the poor of efforts by large donor institutions to use participatory methods in all phases of project and policy development, including design, implementation, monitoring and evaluation;
2   the lessons of experience within donor institutions of the institutional and organizational requirements of promoting genuine 'influence and shared control' over critical decisions about development projects and resource allocations; and
3   the challenges and experiences of the institutional reform process of recipient government implementing agencies to promote and support participation of the poor in all relevant work done by such agencies.

This book examines information presented on the three major themes of the conference. It draws on conference papers and presentations to identify major principles and trends, and to draw lessons from this analysis across a range of experiences. Moreover, the book places the presentations and the results of the conference within the context of efforts made during the past 15 years to promote participation of the poor in development activities. Integrated throughout the book are analyses and commentaries on strategies used by NGOs and others in promoting mainstreaming of participation in the World Bank and, to a lesser extent, in other donor agencies.

Continuing work in incorporating participation goes on as the paradigm for such participation evolves. For some time, there have been two points of view concerning participation. One is an *instrumental* or *functional* view, which holds that participation is a means to an end – that is, participatory practices will result in better projects. The other view is that participation is an end in itself. This view holds that strengthening people's ability to determine how to improve their economic and social conditions is the true essence of development. This is sometimes called the *transformational* view. These two points of view are now converging. Going even beyond this convergence, more and more people are defining participation as a right of citizenship, and as part and parcel of the process of democratization. Indeed, it is increasingly seen – as expressed in the example of Nelson Mandela and the transformation of South Africa – as a fundamental part of people's rights to choose how they are governed and how they, together with their governments, carry out the work of development. This book focuses primarily on the first view – participation as a means to an end – but the other two views involved in this paradigm shift will appear from time to time as they did in the Participation Conference.

THE HISTORICAL CONTEXT

More than 50 years after the World Bank was founded and bilateral aid programmes were started, the imperative of meaningfully involving the poor in their own development has now penetrated the consciousness of donor institutions. What is remarkable is that much of the progress towards this result has been made in the last ten years. Why is this so? What happened to bring this about? What remains to be done to ensure full involvement of the poor in the development process? These questions are treated in the following pages.

In the early days of development, donor agencies, both bilateral and multilateral, were organized and shaped by the understanding that their mission was to *deliver* development to poor countries. People hired by these institutions were trained in economics, engineering or other, mostly technical, disciplines. They were expected to improve economic performance of developing countries, build roads, schools and hospitals, and provide expertise which would improve areas such as health and education.

Development, however, has proven to be a more complex enterprise than anyone visualized in the late 1940s, 1950s, 1960s or even

1970s. Successive development approaches carried out through public multilateral and bilateral organizations have included an early emphasis on economic growth and infrastructural development; a move in the 1970s to meeting basic human needs; the preoccupation in the 1980s with 'getting the prices right' and structural adjustment of developing countries' economies. Development professionals, particularly in donor organizations and government implementing agencies, have struggled to find models and formulae to unleash the potential of developing countries to improve their economic and social conditions. The present-day view holds that economic growth with equity is the appropriate focus, with the understanding that the democratization process, elimination of corruption and more collaboration among donors, governments and civil society are also essential to achieve development results.

It is acknowledged that there have been impressive advances in many sectors in developing countries over the years, including improvements in rates of education, decreases in infant and maternal mortality and morbidity, and increases in life expectancy. Nevertheless, grinding poverty still exists for many. The *Human Development report 1997* noted:

> *more than a quarter of the developing world's people still live in poverty as measured by the human poverty index introduced in this report. About a third – 1.3 billion people – live on income of less than $1 a day.* (United Nations, 1997)

Moreover, the gap between rich and poor continues to widen.

> *The income gap between the fifth of the world's people living in the richest countries and the fifth in the poorest was 74 to 1 in 1997, up from 60 to 1 in 1990 and 30 to 1 in 1960.* (United Nations, 1999, p3)

Although there are many reasons for the difficulties in reducing poverty in countries around the world, one obvious problem lies in the limitations on the involvement of people who know most about what is wrong and how to right it: the poor and marginalized people, themselves.

> *Knowledge for and about development has, for the past fifty years, been so shrouded in economic ideology and burdened with the accoutrements of proof imposed by*

*auditors and academics that it was nearly unthinkable
that it could come from poor people or that it could be
created or used by them.* (Freedman, 1998)

ADOPTION OF PARTICIPATORY PRACTICES

In the early 1970s, the work of participation pioneers such as Paulo
Freire, the famous Brazilian educator, became known around the
world. Freire, who wrote *Pedagogy of the Oppressed*, had worked
with impoverished people in his homeland, and after being expelled
from Brazil, developed a theory for the education of illiterates, particularly adults. His theory was based on the conviction that every
human being, no matter how 'ignorant' or submerged in the 'culture
of silence', is capable of looking critically at his world, and that,
provided with the proper tools, he can gradually perceive his personal
and social reality and deal critically with it. Those who, in learning to
read and write, come to a new awareness of selfhood and begin to
look critically at the social situation in which they find themselves,
often take the initiative in acting to transform the society that has
denied them this opportunity of participation (Freire, 1974).

Freire's work, and that of others engaged in empowering the poor
to change their conditions and shape their own lives, began to be
shared by others and contributed to the early body of knowledge
about popular participation and 'self-reliant' development. Over time,
many participatory processes and tools were created to enable development practitioners to work effectively with the poor:

1 Participatory action research originated in the mid-1970s through
   efforts to combine the organizational sophistication of action
   research with the goal of social transformation of participatory
   research (Brown and Tandon, 1983). Its purpose is to engage the
   poor in research through which they can learn about a problem,
   and then, armed with the knowledge, take action to solve it. It can
   involve both fieldwork and workshops, but unlike participatory
   rural appraisal, which can be done relatively quickly, participatory
   research takes months or years to implement, and emphasizes
   issues of power more than most other methods (Jackson, 1998).
2 Rapid rural appraisal was originally developed in the 1970s and
   1980s as a quick and inexpensive way to involve poor people in
   gathering data for project design. Rapid rural appraisal evolved
   into participatory rural appraisal, which gave poor people author-

ity for generating data themselves (Freedman, 1998). Participatory rural appraisal enables poor people to express and analyse the realities of their lives and conditions, to plan themselves what action to take, and to monitor and evaluate the results (Chambers and Blackburn, 1996).

3 SARAR, developed originally in Indonesia, India and the Philippines in the early 1970s, builds on local knowledge and strengthens local capacity to assess, prioritize, plan, create, organize and evaluate, and is geared particularly to training of local trainers or facilitators. SARAR is an acronym based on five attributes which the approach seeks to build: self-esteem, associative strength, resourcefulness, action planning and responsibility (World Bank, 1996a).

4 Gender analysis, developed in the early 1990s, focuses on understanding and documenting the differences in gender roles, activities, needs and opportunities in a given context (World Bank, 1996a).

For a long time, these approaches and others were used primarily by 'third-sector institutions' (non-profit development organizations, NGOs and community-based organizations for example) and were not adopted for regular use by bilateral or multilateral donor institutions. Perhaps because many NGOs were small, flexible and working directly with poor communities, they were better able to experiment with such approaches than large bureaucratic donor agencies. NGOs and people's organizations achieved impressive results in various places through the use of participatory methodologies. One such example is the Organization of Rural Associations for Progress (ORAP), a people's organization begun at independence in 1980 in Zimbabwe. ORAP, itself, was built through a participatory process of diagnosis, problem-solving and action starting at the family level and linking up through the neighbourhood, community and beyond. By the beginning of 1992, ORAP had one million members in two provinces and, according to its founder, Sithembiso Nyoni, 'had wiped out absolute poverty... all had their basic human needs met' (Nyoni, 1992).

By the latter half of the 1980s, international donor organizations became increasingly open to the participation of the poor in development. Several events and trends seem to have spurred this interest:

• Significant political events were occurring in particular countries, driven largely by people's movements. In the Philippines, the Marcos government was ended by the People's Revolution. Poland was changing, largely as a result of Solidarity, the labour union movement that was the engine of democratization. The Berlin Wall came down. Czechoslovakia and other Central and Eastern European countries opened up, all through significant efforts of people in these countries demanding change.

- NGOs were becoming a more significant force in development. They were recognized for their abilities to work effectively with grassroots communities, and often as an important intermediary between local communities and governments or donors. As of 1990, there were an estimated 50,000 NGOs in developing countries (United Nations, 1993). The number of registered development NGOs in industrialized countries had grown from 1600 in 1980 to 22,970 in 1993 (Edwards and Hulme, 1995). In addition to service delivery, NGOs were mobilizing people to advocate on issues such as gender discrimination, sectoral development policies, environmental concerns and structural adjustment.
- The international women's movement was growing significantly. The Third World Conference on Women in Nairobi in 1985 marked a milestone in the mobilization of women in developing countries who were speaking out for their legal rights and more access to education, health care and employment. The fact that women serve as 'the engine of development' was becoming more and more widely known, as was the pervasive discrimination they suffer.
- The downturn in many economies in the developing world – rising debt, falling terms of trade and the disappointing results of several years of structural adjustment programmes – caused donors to recognize the limitations of macro-economic interventions. They began to pay greater attention to participation as one of the ways to improve development results.

In addition to the trends noted above, more documentation on the value of participation to project effectiveness was becoming available and was getting attention in the donor agencies. For example, a 1985 report from the World Bank's Operations Evaluation Department (OED) documented the link between grassroots participation and project sustainability. (The OED is the World Bank's internal independent evaluation unit that analyses completed projects, mostly in agriculture and rural development.) A USAID study of 52 projects in various sectors, done in 1990, showed a positive correlation between participation and project success which was almost as strong as between the availability of finance and success (Finsterbusch and Van Wicklin, 1987). A United Nations Development Programme (UNDP) – World Bank Water and Sanitation Program study of 121 completed rural water supply projects showed strong associations between overall project effectiveness, sustainability and participation-related variables (Narayan et al, 1995).

Although it had been a long time in coming, the convergence of interest of international donor agencies in the practice of participation between the late 1980s and early 1990s represented the beginning of a sea change in thinking that continues.

ORGANIZATION OF THE BOOK

The following are the subject categories used to report on and analyse progress in incorporating participation of the poor in large donor agencies and recipient government implementing agencies.

The Participants

The principal participants are:

1   *Primary stakeholders:* the poor and marginalized people who are most directly affected by donor-funded initiatives intended to help them. Because they are poor, they are usually not included in decision-making regarding the specific project or policy.
2   *Non-governmental organizations:* private, non-profit voluntary development organizations that engage in one or more of the following activities:
    - direct service delivery to poor individuals or communities;
    - support work such as capacity building, technical assistance and funding to communities, community-based organizations or other NGOs; and
    - advocacy or advocacy-related activities such as research and policy analysis.

They often play an intermediary or linking role between the poor and marginalized, and government or donor organizations. Although they may receive contributions from individuals, they normally do not have memberships or constituencies as do farmers' associations, trade unions or people's movements.

NGOs, trade unions, women's organizations, farmers, academics, human rights groups, community-based organizations and other similar groups together are referred to as *civil society organizations* (meaning non-governmental, private non-profit groups who are expressing themselves and their interests as citizens).

3 *Recipient government implementing agencies*, which are national government ministries or agencies charged with carrying out the development projects funded by the international donor agencies.
4 *Donor agencies*, which are bilateral and multilateral development organizations that provide the funding for projects and formulation of certain development policies. In addition, donor agency staff formulate and design such projects and policies, usually together with recipient government personnel.

Organizational Arrangements

The book looks at important organizational arrangements *between* donor agencies and recipient government implementing agencies, *between* donor agencies and NGOs, and *between* and *among* donor agencies, government implementing agencies, NGOs and the poor. It will also examine reforms and innovations *within* donor agencies and recipient government implementing agencies, such as issues of leadership, human resource development, incentive and reward structures, and systems and procedures.

Important Environmental Factors

National and organizational elements that influence efforts to incorporate participation of the poor include the political, cultural and economic contexts in both the donor agency country and recipient government's country; and political and cultural environments inside donor and recipient organizations as well. Trends in international donor attitudes towards development and actual practices (for example, the use of predetermined project cycles) are examined as to their effects on arrangements between donors and recipient governments and on development results.

Most Important Impacts

Various impacts can be achieved through participatory development initiatives. The most important are the sustainable improvements in social and economic conditions of the poor for whom the initiative is intended. Secondary impacts of great importance include empowerment of the poor to take more active roles in development efforts in their country, increased capacity of all participants to engage in development activities, and progress towards achieving an environment in which democratic development can flourish.

Chapter 2 reviews the evolution of the participation policy in the World Bank and the role NGOs have played in promoting participation in this large, multilateral donor agency. NGOs have played a strategic role in the promotion and monitoring of primary stakeholder participation in many bilateral and multilateral donor agencies. Because more NGOs have promoted participation at the World Bank than at any other donor agency, however, this in-depth analysis focuses on the World Bank. The chapter describes the process of engagement between NGOs and the World Bank during the past decade and analyses how such engagement influenced the World Bank as it made efforts to incorporate participation into its operations. Through this 'case study', principles and lessons are drawn concerning this insider/outsider approach towards organizational change.

Chapter 3 examines progress achieved in incorporating participation of the poor into projects and policy development processes. This is done through an examination of the experiences of three multilateral and bilateral donor agencies, as well as through the Working Group's direct experience in monitoring reports on World Bank-funded projects and policy formulation processes. Drawing on experiences of GTZ, DFID, and the World Bank, the chapter reviews efforts to use various kinds of participation at different stages of the project cycle, and the brief but important history of participation in policy formulation processes. Beginning in earnest only about four years ago, such consultations with civil society organizations and, in some instances, the poor themselves, represent an important shift in thinking about the use and importance of participation. Participatory mechanisms and how they are used, and should be used, are reviewed. The chapter also notes changes necessary in the project cycle and process of policy formulation if participation is to be mutually beneficial and effective for all concerned.

In Chapter 4, the record of experience of two international donor agencies in incorporating the participation of the poor is analysed in detail. The orientation in this discussion is towards organizational reforms and innovations necessary to enable the full incorporation of participation into the operations of donor agencies. Experiences of the World Bank and USAID are analysed and contrasted, given their different organizational approaches. These two donor agencies were chosen based on detailed reports presented by each on organizational change at the 1998 Participation Conference. The chapter reviews reform of internal organizational elements such as leadership, incentive and reward structures, human resource development, and systems and procedures. In addition, the roles and importance of governance structures for donor agencies, as well as the record in creating accountability mechanisms, is reviewed.

Organizational reforms and innovations needed in recipient government implementing agencies are treated in Chapter 5. Just as donor agencies that intend to incorporate participation need to reorganize their structures and procedures, so also do government ministries and other implementing agencies in Southern governments. Using the limited written record of such experiences, lessons learned regarding the important elements of an enabling environment for government implementing agencies, as well as actual experiences undertaken to transform such agencies or specific large development projects, are examined. In terms of the enabling environment, the chapter looks at external factors such as the changing donor development paradigm, current donor attention to topics previously considered overtly political (for example, democracy and governance issues) and changing roles of participants in development. Internal factors in a country such as political culture, decentralization, and growing demand for citizen participation, and how these elements influence implementation agencies and their behaviour are also examined. Various experiences of organizational change in several countries are reviewed, focusing on what must be changed in order to incorporate participation. Last, the chapter notes how donor agencies can change their own practices to assist Southern governments to institutionalize participation.

Finally, Chapter 6 summarizes the major themes and findings from the experiences of the past ten years and from these experiences distills lessons to guide future efforts in the participation of the poor. This synthesis of lessons learned regarding attitudinal changes and experiences in practice, as well as in organizational reforms and innovations, sets the stage for charting a way forward in the participation of the poor. This will concern not only how participation can be carried out in projects and policy development processes in the future, but also how large donor agencies and recipient government implementing agencies can effectively reform themselves in order to incorporate participation.

DEFINITIONS AND FOCUS

As we begin a review of donor efforts in promoting participation of the poor, it is important to use basic terms in a consistent way. The terms *participation*, *popular participation*, and *participatory development* are often used quite loosely, and sometimes interchangeably. *Webster's English Dictionary* defines participate as 'to take or have a part'. The synonym is 'to share' (Webster's Dictionary, 1996). Thus the inclusive nature of participation is evident in this most basic of definitions.

The World Bank's definition of *participation* is '... a process through which stakeholders influence and share control over their own development initiatives, decisions, and resources which affect them' (World Bank, 1994b).

When beginning its monitoring of World Bank-funded projects and policy formulation processes in 1995, the Working Group amended the World Bank's definition to put an emphasis on those who are poor and marginalized, that is, primary stakeholders. The reasoning for this was that the World Bank's definition 'clubs together all stakeholders, ignoring inequalities which affect the ability of different stakeholders, particularly those who are poor and marginalized, to take part effectively in decision-making' (Tandon and Cordeiro, 1998). Most NGOs involved in monitoring donor efforts in participation favour a definition of participation that characterizes the poor as playing a more assertive and central decision-making role. This book specifically examines large donor agencies and their efforts. Because the World Bank's experience is the primary focus of this book and for purposes of uniformity, we use the World Bank definition as amended by the Working Group, which reads as follows: '... a process through which *primary* stakeholders influence and share control over their own development initiatives, decisions, and resources which affect them' (Tandon and Cordeiro, 1998). Box 1.1 gives definitions of participation from the other donor agencies included in this book.

Two other important terms that will be used in this book are *stakeholder* and *mainstreaming*. Among the myriad definitions of the word *stake* in *Webster's English Dictionary*, the clearest in relation to development is 'a monetary or businesslike interest, investment, share or involvement in something as in hope of gain' (Webster's Dictionary, 1996).

Among the donors, there are differences regarding the definition of *stakeholder*. The World Bank has this to say about stakeholders:

> *Key stakeholders are clearly those intended to be directly affected by a proposed intervention, ie, those who may be expected to benefit or lose from Bank-supported operations; or who warrant redress from any negative effects of such operations, particularly among the poor and marginalized. Those indirectly involved or affected can include persons or institutions (1) with technical expertise and public interest in Bank-supported policies and programs; and (2) with linkages to the poor and marginalized. Such stakeholders may include NGOs,*

Box 1.1 Definitions of Participation by Donor Agencies

DFID: 'Participatory approaches take into account the views and needs of the poor, and tackle disparities between men and women throughout society' (Feeney, 1998).

GTZ: The GTZ definition of participation is evolving.

> *To date, rather a functional view predominates. Participation is seen as a principle to promote initiative, self-determination and the taking over of responsibility by beneficiaries, thus representing a critical factor for meeting a project's objectives. Increasingly, however, it is felt insufficient to establish participation on a 'project island'. The term [has to be] understood as a socio-political process concerning the relationships between different stakeholders in a society, such as social groups, community, policy level and service delivering institutions. In this meaning participation aims at an increase in self-determination and a re-adjustment of control over development initiatives and resources.* (Forster, 1998)

Sida: 'Popular participation in Swedish development cooperation can be viewed with reference to the democracy and equity goals, as an objective in itself – that is, a basic democratic right that should be promoted in all development projects. It is also considered a means of increasing efficiency, effectiveness, and sustainability in development projects' (Rudqvist, 1992).

USAID: 'The active engagement of partners and customers in sharing ideas, committing time and resources, making decisions, and taking action to bring about a desired development objective' (USAID, 1995).

---

various intermediary or representative organizations, private sector businesses and technical and professional bodies. (World Bank, 1996a)

On the other hand, USAID defines *stakeholders* in this way:

USAID uses the term 'stakeholder' to refer to 'those individuals and/or groups who exercise some type of authority over USAID resources such as Congress, Office of Management and Budget, Department of State, and those who influence the political process, eg, interest groups and taxpayers...' USAID also recognizes that 'stakeholders' in the field include a full range of actors,

---

BOX 1.2 PARTICIPATION MECHANISMS

1   Information-sharing mechanisms
- Translation into local languages and dissemination of written material using various media
- Informational seminars, presentations and public meetings

2   Consultative mechanisms
- Consultative meetings
- Field visits and interviews (at various stages of the work)

3   Joint assessment mechanisms
- Participatory assessments and evaluations
- Beneficiary assessment

4   Shared decision-making mechanisms
- Participatory planning techniques
- Workshops and retreats to discuss and determine positions, priorities, roles
- Meetings to help resolve conflicts, seek agreements, engender ownership
- (Public) reviews of draft documents and subsequent revisions

5   Collaborative mechanisms
- Formation of joint committees with stakeholder representatives
- Formation of joint working groups, task forces
- Joint work with user groups, intermediary organizations, and other stakeholder groups
- Stakeholder groups given principal responsibility for implementation

6   Empowering mechanisms
- Capacity-building of stakeholder organizations
- Strengthening the financial and legal status of stakeholder organizations
- Hand-over and self-management by stakeholders
- Support for new, spontaneous initiatives by stakeholders (World Bank, 1994b).

---

including customers and partners and those who may be adversely affected by, or represent opposition to, development efforts. (La Voy and Charles, 1998)

This book will use the World Bank's definition of stakeholders. The term *primary stakeholders* will be used to refer to poor and marginalized people (frequently referred to simply as 'the poor'). The term *secondary stakeholders* will be used to refer to people indirectly involved with, or affected by, projects or policies. Among others, these can include staff of recipient or borrower government implementing agencies, or NGOs or others with linkages to the poor and marginalized.

BOX 1.3 PROJECT CYCLE

1 *Identification phase.* Also called the *formulation phase* by some donors, this is the information-gathering phase. During this time, the donor and/or government representatives or their consultants assess various aspects of an intended project. These include a determination of how the intended project will contribute to economic development, poverty alleviation, or a specific goal within a sector, such as improvement in primary health care or basic education; who will benefit from the project; and how it will affect local populations for example. This identification is based partly on information from such sources as earlier policy work or feasibility studies, in the case of the World Bank or USAID, or proposals developed by the recipient government, in the case of GTZ.

2 *Design phase.* Also called the *preparation phase* or *project planning phase*, this is when the project, itself, is designed by the government, the donor or both. It is shaped into a fully-fledged proposal, complete with technical, economic, social, institutional and other factors. In the case of the World Bank, following this phase an appraisal takes place in which World Bank staff and consultants determine the viability of the project and the capacity of the implementing agencies. These findings and recommendations form the basis for a staff appraisal report, which is reviewed by the World Bank and then forms the basis for negotiations with the recipient government.

3 *Implementation phase.* Once the project has been agreed between the donor and the recipient government and money has begun to be disbursed, the implementation phase begins. This is when the actual project is carried out.

4 *Evaluation.* This phase includes monitoring, which is to go on during the project at regular intervals. Feedback from such monitoring should be used to make corrections in the project. Evaluation is normally carried out at the end of the project or some time after the completion date to determine the success of the project in meeting its objectives and achieving results.

(World Bank, 1996b).

The term *mainstream* is defined by Webster's as 'the principal or dominant course, tendency, or trend' (Webster's Dictionary, 1996). The World Bank has used the word *mainstreaming* since 1994 to describe its efforts to integrate participation into operations but has never defined the term precisely. USAID has said:

> *By 'mainstreaming', we refer principally to making more routine those practices by us, as donor institutions and development implementing organizations, whose effect is the fuller engagement of people in their society's decision-making processes.* (La Voy and Charles, 1998)

This book uses a definition of *mainstreaming* that has been implicit in the work of the Working Group: it is the full and systematic incorporation of a particular issue into the work of an organization so that it becomes an accepted and regular part of the organization's policies and practices.

The next set of definitions pertains to the kinds of participation that are used in project or policy formulation and the different stages of project development to which these participatory methodologies are applied. During the deliberations of the Learning Group, six participatory mechanisms used in World Bank-funded project and policy work were delineated and are used throughout this book (see Box 1.2). They represent a clear continuum of stakeholder involvement.

Generally speaking, the first three categories are viewed as *instrumental* participation (a means to an end, that is, will result in a better project). The second three are viewed as *transformational* participation (an end in themselves which, of course, should also result in a better project). In many ways, the first three categories are preconditions for participation in that they prepare the way for the final three to occur. Information sharing, consultations and joint assessment lay the groundwork for the poor to become involved in joint decision-making and collaboration, and, having been empowered, continue on to improve their social and economic conditions.

Of the five donors whose work is discussed in this book, Sida and USAID have abandoned use of the project cycle in favour of more flexible project development methodologies intended to remove organizational barriers to participation and increase prospects for programme success. The World Bank, GTZ and DFID continue to focus primary attention on participation as practised in the various phases of the project cycle, that is, the period of time during which a project is first identified, then designed in more detail, negotiated with the recipient government, implemented, monitored and evaluated. These are artificial phases created for bureaucratic purposes to ensure that projects are ready for review at predetermined points in an organization's calendar. These donor-determined phases often conflict with the natural progression of a project's development. For purposes of description and analysis, we use the donor project cycles in this book. There are four or five major phases in any donor's project cycle. For simplicity, we use the four major categories outlined in Box 1.3.

Chapter 2

The World Bank and NGOs: The Evolution of a Participation Policy

INTRODUCTION

This chapter focuses on the development and evolution of the World Bank's participation policy over an 11-year period from 1987 to 1998 as well as the process of engagement between the Bank and NGOs. It analyses how such engagement influenced the Bank in its efforts to incorporate participation into its operations. This documentation and analysis of NGO–Bank engagement regarding participation represents one major example of a long-term effort by NGOs to persuade and assist a major international donor agency to incorporate a significant change in its practice of development.

This chapter examines the role of NGOs generally in influencing the World Bank, but pays particular attention to the Working Group as the principal long-term NGO advocate on participation. How and why the Bank took up the topic of participation is integrally related to the interaction of the Working Group with the World Bank. Thus, in order to tell the story of one, one must tell the story of the other.

BACKGROUND

In 1987, when the topic of participation was first proposed for examination at the Bank, the environment in the institution was changing as a result of several important political events. The Cold War was winding down and support to 'client' dictators of the superpowers was dwindling as a result. The Bank was being pressured less by the United States and other important industrialized countries to lend to such countries. The US failure in Vietnam had weakened its foreign policy leadership, and the United States and a few other Northern governments were seen as having slightly less influence at the Bank than was previously the case. Thus, the political landscape was shifting. Moreover, important changes were occurring in several countries as a result of people's own actions. Poland was changing largely as a result of the efforts led by Solidarity, the labour union that was the principal engine of democratization there. In the Philippines, the Marcos government was being ended by the 'People's Revolution'. Both of these major changes went on without any foreign support; in fact, in the Philippines, it happened in spite of it! Democratic changes were also beginning in Brazil.

At this time, NGOs were lobbying the Bank on three major issues:

1   to halt negative environmental and social impacts of large Bank-funded projects;
2   to establish an information disclosure policy; and
3   to stop structural adjustment programmes that were harming the poor.

Since the early 1980s, NGOs were becoming an increasingly important external force affecting the Bank. Their influence was most visible in the efforts by environmentalists to change Bank projects and policies. This work was started in 1983, primarily by a small group of Washington-based environmentalists. These activists, based in large membership organizations (such as the Environmental Defense Fund, the Sierra Club and the National Wildlife Federation), used the domestic political clout of their millions of dues-paying members to pressure the US Congress and the US Treasury to call for Bank reforms. Because the United States was its largest donor until 1997, it had significant leverage with its management. By the time the topic of participation was first raised in 1987, environmental advocacy efforts had already led to the creation of an Environmental Department at the organization that year. A second Bank reform took place in 1989 when an environmental assessment policy was put in place. By this time, advocacy groups in developing countries as well as NGO campaigns in other industrialized countries had begun to play leading roles. In the years since participation has been taken up by the Bank, environmental activism has continued and intensified around the world, has involved a variety of NGO and grassroots participants and has continued to be directed at particular projects as well as policy reform (Fox and Brown, 1998).

NGO advocacy regarding information disclosure grew directly out of the environmental campaigns, and it was the first participation issue taken up by NGOs. This long-term effort to create a transparent bank achieved partial success in 1993 and continues until the present day. Another initiative that grew out of environmental advocacy on specific projects was a call for an inspection panel, which was established in 1994. This is a relatively autonomous appeals mechanism through which people directly affected by a Bank-funded project can call for an investigation as to whether its policies have been violated in the course of the project cycle. Comprehensive treatment of NGO advocacy campaigns on the environment, information disclosure and the inspection panel at the World Bank can be found in two books, *The Struggle for Accountability* (Fox and Brown, 1998) and *Beyond Borders* (Keck and Sikkink, 1998).

These intense and expanding global NGO environmental advocacy efforts in the1980s created the political context at the Bank into which participation was introduced. By 1987 the Working Group had raised the question of popular participation and information disclosure as preconditions for meaningful civil society participation. (Themes taken up consistently throughout the life of this group have included promoting civil society, especially Southern, voices in Bank policies and projects; ameliorating the negative development and social impacts of structural adjustment; and monitoring the nature of NGO–Bank relationships themselves) (Covey, 1998).

During Robert MacNamara's tenure as World Bank president, from 1968 to 1981, the institution began paying attention to poverty for the first time. However, during the term of the next president, Alden Clausen, (1981–1986), the attention to poverty was forsaken. Instead, there were concerns about the oil crisis. During that time, the Bank also began its structural adjustment programmes. Barber Conable, a former US congressional representative, took over as it president in mid-1986. After Conable's arrival, task forces were created to regenerate interest in poverty, but such efforts were getting nowhere. Conable was sympathetic to NGOs calling for changes in the way Bank projects were designed and implemented because of the damage the projects caused to the environment. Conable called the NGOs the 'eyes and ears of the World Bank' and understood that some sort of engagement with grassroots people could help it be more accountable.

In 1987, a meeting was held at the Bank with a variety of Northern NGOs, some of which had been advocating changes at the Bank (see Table 2.1). These included environmental and development organizations, church-related groups and secular organizations, and those that carried out operations as well as those that were primarily or exclusively policy advocates. The NGOs were invited to discuss how the Bank might engage constructively with them on issues of importance. Bank staff and NGO representatives present at that meeting reached a consensus that the Bank should collaborate with local NGOs in developing countries on the grounds that their influence would help to link it more effectively with poor and marginalized people in client countries. This had been advocated in earlier NGO–Bank Committee discussions. Present at that meeting was Bill Stanton, who worked in President Conable's office. He affirmed the interest of the president in this issue. Stanton's support was particularly important given events going on at the Bank. President Conable had just undertaken a major reorganization. In fact, on the day of the NGO meeting, all new division chiefs were being appointed, and Bank staff didn't know if they still had their jobs. To say the least, it was a tense time.

At the next meeting of the NGO–Bank Committee in Santo Domingo, Dominican Republic in March 1987, participants discussed Bank collaboration with local NGOs. This collaboration became a major part of the *Consensus Document* agreed to at that meeting. The *Consensus Document* recognized the importance of including Southern knowledge and experience in programme and policy formulation, and identified policy dialogue as an explicit purpose of the committee. This document also refined the committee's operating mechanisms in order to expand the role of Southern members. For example, it proposed regular member-organized consultations at national and regional levels to enhance direct Southern consultations with the Bank. Only one NGO, the Association of Voluntary Agencies for Rural Development (AVARD) in India was successful in forming a consultation committee that held regular meetings with Bank representatives (Covey, 1998).

Following the Santo Domingo meeting, Alex Shakow, the new director of strategic planning under the reorganization, who had just taken over as the Bank co-chair of the NGO–Bank committee said about the *Consensus Document*, 'We'll push this.' A former member of staff at the Bank at the time said of Shakow's commitment: 'That was gutsy'.

HISTORY OF PARTICIPATION INITIATIVE

The Strategic Planning Division with an NGO unit was set up in the Bank as part of the reorganization. Although the unit's work would be to liaise with all NGOs, the Bank's decision to engage with Southern NGOs was seen as a significant mandate.

Table 2.1 *Main events related to participation at the World Bank*

Year	Events
1987	*February* World Bank meeting with Northern NGOs.
1988	*March* NGO–Bank Steering Committee meeting, Rome, Italy. Discussion about how to determine committee's agenda.
1989	*March* NGO–Bank Committee meeting, Bangkok, Thailand. Discussion about structural adjustment, participation.
1990	*December* World Bank Learning Group on Popular Participation launched.
1991	*March* NGO–Bank Steering Committee meeting, Saly, Senegal. *Saly Declaration* written by NGOs. Creation of Working Group Subgroup on Participation.
1992	*February* First World Bank workshop on participation.
1994	*May* Second and final World Bank workshop on participation.
1995	*March* Regional participation action plans prepared. *April* participation. First and only Senior Oversight Committee meeting. *March and October* Working Group reactivates Subgroup on Participation.
1996	*July* NGO–Bank seminar on participation. *September* Inter-Agency Group on Participation begins to lose momentum. *October* First meeting of Working Group with Bank board of directors.
1997	*February* Working Group launches 18-month monitoring process. *March* FIAHS eliminated when *Strategic Compact* adopted.
1998	*November* Participation Conference held at World Bank.

Table 2.1 *continued*

1987	1988	1989	1990	1991	1992	1994	1995	1996	1997	1998
March NGO–Bank Committee meeting, Santo Domingo, Dominican Republic: *Consensus Document*.					*May–July* Mid-term report of Learning Group on Popular Participation prepared.	*July* Fund for Innovative Approaches in Human and Social Development (FIAHS) created.	Inter-Agency Group on Participation meets. *March* Working Group Development Group decentralizes monitoring. meetings.	*October* Working Group adopts strategy re participation		
						September Final report of Learning Group approved by Bank board.	*December* 'Presidential flagships' announced.	*December* 'Presidential flagships' eliminated.		

The work programme of the NGO unit encompassed three major issues: operational collaboration with Southern NGOs, listening to NGOs regarding poverty and structural adjustment and learning about a new, important development issue and how it relates to the work of the Bank. As part of the process of choosing which development issue to study, the Unit members sought input from inside the Bank as well as from the Working Group.

The topic that NGO Unit staff thought would be appropriate to study was popular participation, defined at the International Conference at Arusha, Tanzania, as:

> *the empowerment of the people to effectively involve themselves in creating the structures and in designing policies and programmes that serve the interests of all as well as to effectively contribute to the development process and share equitably in its benefits.* (African Charter, 1990)

At that time, a few Bank staff and consultants were writing books and papers noting the importance of participation of the poor in development: *Putting People First: Sociological Variables in Rural Development* (Cernea, 1985), *Listen to the People* (Salmen, 1987), *The Role of Community Participation in Development Planning and Project Management* (Bamberger, 1998) and *Community Participation in Development Projects: The World Bank Experience* (Paul, 1987) all contributed to lobbying efforts inside the Bank for more attention to this topic. In addition, at that time the OED was discussing evidence showing that participation of the poor was linked to project effectiveness. The Bank, however, knew very little about how to carry out participatory work.

Another important influence at that time was the publication of the book: *Transforming a Bureaucracy: The Experience of the Philippine National Irrigation Administration* which documented how the National Irrigation Administration (NIA) created and implemented its participatory programme (Korten and Siy, 1988). Because this was a large-scale effort in a government implementing agency, it was seen as particularly relevant to the work of the World Bank.

According to a member of the Working Group at that time, the Bank took up the issue of popular participation as a result of the lobbying, pressure and discussion that NGOs had had with them. 'We were talking about participation and the Bank got into it because everyone else was doing it'.

At the Rome meeting, the topic of popular participation was broached for the first time. The Bank representatives asked the NGOs for input on whether it should create an initiative. The NGOs greeted this request initially with a lack of interest because they were so intent on engaging the Bank on structural adjustment and its damaging effects on the poor – to whom the Bank had no real connection. A member of the Working Group at that time characterized the dialogue this way: 'Bank officials listened to what we said but you had the feeling they weren't really taking it in ... and that they weren't going to do anything with the information. It felt like a public relations exercise. There was inconsistent attendance by Bank staff and new faces at each meeting. Ismail Serageldin was the one exception. He came to all our meetings, listened and was genuinely prepared to take action.'[1]

At the next full meeting of the committee in Bangkok, Thailand in 1989, a heated discussion on structural adjustment took place, with no common ground on the topic being found. Bank participants raised, again, the topic of popular participation. Some of the Southern NGO leaders, in particular Fasle Abed and Mazide N'Diaye, spoke on the topic. Abed is founder of the Bangladesh Rural Advancement Committee (BRAC), and N'Diaye is founder of the African Network for Integrated Development/Réseau Africain pour le Développement Intègre (RADI) and founder of the pan-African network, Forum of African Voluntary Development Organizations (FAVDO). Both had had long experience with participation in grass-roots development initiatives in their own countries and cautioned the Bank to proceed carefully and slowly. They advised against announcing any major initiative. They warned that participatory approaches were difficult to carry out, didn't always succeed, and could result in damage to local institutions if not done properly. The experience of the NGOs on the committee had been with small-scale participation efforts. The Bank was interested in how to carry out participation in large-scale projects. It turned out that almost no one knew how to carry out participatory initiatives on a large scale.

Given the cautionary advice of the NGOs and the lack of information available on participation of the poor in large-scale projects, Bank staff decided to proceed by proposing a learning group on the topic. NGOs were enthusiastic and supportive of the initiative.

Following the discussion with the NGOs in Bangkok, it was proposed that the Bank set up a Learning Group on Popular Participation. There were two precedents for the Learning Group:

1   The 'Friday Morning Group,' a voluntary group of Bank staff interested in the links between development and spirituality, which lobbied for greater Bank attention to poverty.[2]

2   Respect for the learning strategy approach used in the successful transformation of the Philippine NIA.[3]

There was resistance to the concept, however, and speculation about the sources of resistance centred on issues such as:

*   the character of certain governments that had centrally-run economies and were unresponsive to such 'Western' ideas;
*   the concern by Bank staff that this was one more development trend ('flavour of the month') they would have to discuss with busy finance ministers;
*   simple inertia and resistance to change;
*   feasibility of such an initiative in countries with poorly functioning or non-existent parliaments where the Bank's effort might be perceived as a new kind of imperialism; and
*   task managers' attitudes that they didn't have enough resources allocated for projects without participation, let alone with it.

In spite of the lack of support, Moeen Qureshi, who was senior vice president of operations at the time, ultimately approved the idea. As one former Bank staffer involved in the effort recalls: 'He [Qureshi] was our patron at the highest level ... but the political support for it was so tentative inside the Bank that without the external NGO influence, someone could have shut it down'.

The Learning Group and Policy Adoption

The Learning Group was launched in December 1990. Its mandate was to 'examine the issue of participation and identify challenges to the Bank in stepping up its efforts to support participation in its operations' (World Bank, 1994). Twelve to fifteen committed innovators comprised the core Learning Group. They chose 20 projects to examine and analysed them in terms of participation issues as well as the Bank's capacity to support such participation.[4] Funds for the work of the group were made available from a trust fund provided by Sida. GTZ provided additional assistance later in the life of the Learning Group's work. Both Sida and GTZ had committed themselves to participation earlier: Sida in 1981 and GTZ in 1986.

The Learning Group organized a workshop in February 1992. In order to benefit from outside experience and expertise, half the participants were drawn from outside the Bank (including NGOs, academics and representatives of other development agencies) and half from inside the Bank. The workshop analysed experiences of other agencies in participation and country constraints, and focused

---

Box 2.1 NGO Addendum to the World Bank's Participation Report

The World Bank's participation report included an 'Addendum to the Report of the Participatory Development Learning Group' prepared by a group of NGO representatives who had been participants in the final workshop of the Learning Group held in May 1994. The addendum made a number of observations about the Learning Group's report and recommendations. It included its own recommendations, of which the following four were central:

1 Put heavier emphasis on participation by poor people who are often bypassed by development.
2 Rethink the project cycle.
3 Take a 'transformational' approach to participation by engaging and empowering communities to set development priorities. This approach contrasts with the 'instrumental' approach through which the donor basically engages in social marketing of its operational plans.
4 Acknowledge that the Bank, itself, is a stakeholder (Alexander et al, 1994).[5]

---

on how to understand better the Bank's particular constraints to participation of the poor (Bhatnagar and Williams, 1992).

Although originally planned for three years, the Learning Group existed for four, and completed its final report and recommendations in September 1994. The report, entitled *The World Bank and Participation*, included an action plan called 'Immediate Actions to Mainstream Current Bank Work on Participation'.

The Board approved the full report, including the action plan, in September 1994. This report became the closest thing to a participation policy that the Bank has had up to and including the present.

NGO Involvement During the Learning Group Period

During the life of the Learning Group, NGOs worked to influence and promote the work on participation being done at the Bank. Early in the process, in 1990, members of the Working Group advocated a stronger definition of participation than the one the Bank was using – one with an emphasis on demand-driven participation which would involve the poor in pro-active ways, including decision-making roles throughout the project cycle. NGOs advocated information-sharing and consultation but emphasized that these were important *preconditions* for meaningful participation.

With regard to groups targeted for participation, the Bank's use of the term *stakeholder* included borrower governments, business, civil society and the poor who were intended beneficiaries of the particular project. NGOs urged a primary focus on the poor as the most important stakeholder group.

In March 1991, at the NGO–World Bank Steering Committee meeting in Saly, Senegal, the NGOs wrote the *Saly Declaration*. This statement did two important things:

1   It stated that the two highest priorities of the Working Group, henceforth, would be popular participation and structural adjustment. Subgroups were formed to work on each of these topics.
2   The Working Group explicitly defined itself as an autonomous advocacy mechanism for promoting World Bank reform (NGO Working Group, 1991). (Although the 1987 *Consensus Document* had identified policy dialogue as a purpose of the Committee, until the Saly meeting the Bank had viewed the Committee only as a mechanism for information sharing and dialogue. It did not see the Working Group as a channel for NGO advocacy on Bank policy).

Bank President Lewis Preston, who had taken over the reins from Barber Conable in August 1991, chose the October 1992 meeting of the NGO–World Bank Committee as the platform to express his personal commitment to making the practice of popular participation an issue in which the whole Bank structure should be involved (Arruda, 1993).

Also in 1992, NGO advocates for information disclosure and the establishment of an inspection panel (see later in this chapter) clashed with other NGOs working on participation over the issue of International Development Association (IDA) replenishment. The IDA is the Bank's soft loan window, but only the poorest developing countries are eligible for assistance. IDA loans have maturities of 35 or 40 years with a 10-year grace period on repayment of principal. There is no interest charge, but credits do carry a small service charge. The bulk of IDA resources is contributed by the governments of more than 30 donor countries who come together every three years to decide on the amount of new resources to be transferred to poor countries and on the priorities for the use of these resources (World Bank, 1997). IDA deputies are the individuals designated by the executive branches of donor governments to negotiate the replenishment with the Bank. As such, they represent an advocacy target for NGOs interested in Bank reform. The parliaments of these donor governments, or the Congress in the case of the United States, can also be advocacy targets since they vote to approve the funding recommendations of their governments' executive branches.

BOX 2.2 NGO STATEMENT AT WORLD BANK'S PARTICIPATION WORKSHOP, FEBRUARY 1992

The Bank invited five representatives from the Working Group as participants in the February 1992 workshop on participation, together with eight other NGO participants. The Working Group was given the opportunity to make a statement about the progress of the Learning Group. The statement specifically urged the Bank to:

1   Focus more on transformational (demand-driven) aspects of participation.
2   Change its procedures (eg the project cycle) which impede adoption of participatory practices in the organization.
3   Have senior Bank officials give recognition to participation 'pioneers' within the organization.
4   'Walk the talk'; that is, practise participation in project and policy development processes with borrower governments.
5   Begin to formulate structural adjustment programmes in a participatory way (Long, 1992).

In 1992, a group of Indian and other Asian and international NGOs who had worked together to stop Bank funding of the Narmada Dam in India used the oversight and funding authority of the Northern donor governments for IDA (especially the US Congress) as a tool to win adoption of a new information disclosure policy and the establishment of the inspection panel at the World Bank. Focusing specifically on the United States, a group of US NGOs, largely drawn from the environmental movement, urged the US Congress not to authorize the US$3.7 billion for the tenth IDA replenishment until the Bank agreed to adopt the two reforms.

As that campaign gathered momentum, worried Bank officials invited Southern NGO representatives (including four from the Working Group) to a September 1992 meeting in Washington, DC, to discuss IDA funding and needed Bank reforms. Rather than calling for cuts in IDA funding if reforms were not made, the NGO representatives called for reforms and full funding for IDA. An African NGO representative, together with US development NGO allies, also met with a US legislator who was a key figure in the replenishment debate. The NGO co-chair of the NGO–Bank Committee signed a letter to Bank President Lewis Preston. The letter 'calls for full IDA 10 replenishment[6] and future funding at increased levels; asserts that IDA funds should not be used for structural adjustment and that popular participation should become a Bank priority; and supports the broad NGO campaign for greater accountability and participation in the use of IDA funds, but cautions that protection of the global environment should not be accomplished by diminishing efforts to reduce poverty' (Covey, 1998). The Working Group stopped short of demanding specific action by the Bank as a quid pro quo for replenishment.

This stance by the Working Group caused tensions within the NGO community:

> ...*Some NGO advocates also interpret it as a 'divide-and-conquer' tactic by the Bank in which the NGO Working Group position was held out as 'more legitimate' because it was rooted in Southern NGO views. Generally, Southern NGOs with a poverty focus feel that the episode simply revealed the diversity of NGO interests and concerns. Certainly, it highlights the fact that NGOs working on World Bank reform have different priorities and different strategies that are sometimes in conflict (at least in the short term) with one another* (Covey, 1998)

In May 1992, as Bank staff were preparing the mid-term report to Bank management to be submitted in August 1992, they asked members of the Working Group for comments on the draft report. The Working Group response noted that the report was silent on the need for the Bank to undertake *fundamental* organizational changes in order to incorporate participation of the poor. The NGOs urged that the Bank adopt new personnel incentives and rewards linked to participation, carry out training of staff, and alter the project cycle and other procedures that were impediments to participatory practices (InterAction, 1992). The final mid-term report included a recommendation for training (later carried out) but not the other changes urged by the Working Group.

The Bank held a second and final workshop in May 1994 in which approximately 30 NGO representatives participated. Some of the NGO participants wrote an addendum to the Learning Group's report, which was included in the final published version (see Box 2.1).

In addition to the addendum's recommendations, a small group of NGOs urged creation of a senior management committee to oversee implementation of the action plan in the Bank's report. This suggestion was accepted and included in the final report; and the committee was formed following Board approval of the report and action plan in September 1994.

Reflections on the Learning Group Period and the Role Played by NGOs

Participation advocates throughout the development community generally viewed the Bank's four-year Learning Group experience as an impressive effort to lay the groundwork for incorporation of participatory practices into its operations. The research and analysis of the Bank's own efforts at participation, the circulation of its papers on the work of the Learning Group and the wide outreach to many outside the Bank who understood and practised participation all contributed to the success of the endeavour. Carried out as it was in an uncharacteristically humble way, the organization's efforts were warmly received by outsiders. The workshops and openness to input by outsiders exhibited by the Participation Coordinator and Learning Group members ensured that the Bank engaged seriously with knowledgeable people on this topic.[7]

The report, *The World Bank and Participation* (World Bank, 1994b), reveals an excellent understanding of participation of the poor in its various aspects gained from the four years of study. The report also clearly presents the results of the Learning Group's review of the Bank's own experience in participation, as well as both a long-term strategy and an immediate action plan to incorporate participatory practices into its operations.

The NGO addendum to the 1994 report represented the first time a set of comments and recommendations written by outsiders was included in a Bank report prepared for the Board and published.

In 1998, Aubrey Williams wrote a reflection paper on the Learning Group. Williams had served as Participation Coordinator during the life of the Learning Group and the implementation phase of the action plan until 1997. He noted that although the central work of the group was to be the 21 projects chosen at the beginning, that focus had had limited usefulness because the projects had not been analysed with uniform methodological rigour. Rather, some of the best learning came from dialogue within the group itself, with outsiders and through the workshops. Moreover, connections made with people involved in other Bank task forces who appreciated the Learning Group's work advanced the topic. For example, Dominique Lallement of the Wapenhans Task Force (discussed below) promoted participation of the poor. A few senior Bank managers also played key roles. Robert Picciotto, now director general of the OED, was initially a sceptic, feeling the Bank was already engaged in participatory development. He later changed his view and became a strong ally.[8] Sven Sandstrom, a managing director, thought the topic was being constrained by a small learning group. To expand its reach, in

1992, he promoted additional support mechanisms such as a participation fund, training, bringing in eminent outside speakers to convince the sceptics of the value of participation of the poor, and contracting with consultants to examine particular Bank procedures that were constraining efforts to work with grassroots communities (Williams, 1998).

Although not focused on participation, another major Bank undertaking during the period of the Learning Group contributed to the recognition that changes in Bank operations were needed. The Task Force on Portfolio Management reviewed the implementation success of the organization's entire project portfolio and produced the 'Wapenhans Report' transmitted to the executive directors on 3 November 1992. The report observed systemic deficiencies in project quality and implementation, and an increase in projects with 'major problems' – from 11 per cent of projects in 1981 to 20 per cent in 1991. The number of projects judged unsatisfactory at completion increased from 15 per cent of those reviewed in 1981 to 37.5 per cent of those reviewed in 1991 (World Bank, 1992, quoted in Udall, 1998).

In other words, 'more than a third of all Bank projects were considered failures by its own criteria' (Gray, 1998). According to the report, the reason for this was a pervasive 'approval culture' inside the Bank: staff perceived project appraisals as internal 'marketing devices' for securing loan approval and achieving personal recognition (World Bank, 1992, quoted in Udall, 1998). Lending money was what was driving Bank behaviour, not project quality. Noting the fundamental nature of the problem, the report said ' ... the pressure is not temporary, it is attributable to deep-rooted problems which must be diagnosed and resolved. The cost of tolerating continued poor performance is highest not for the Bank, but for its borrowers' (World Bank, 1992, quoted in Udall, 1998).

In response to the report, the Bank developed a new management approach to development projects and an action plan outlined in *Getting Results: The World Bank's Agenda for Improving Development Effectiveness* (World Bank, 1993). Two of the major areas dealt with in the report were efforts to improve the quality of projects entering the portfolio and the need to give attention to generic and institutional factors that affect portfolio performance. These topics provided openings for a discussion of the need for participation of the poor in the Bank's operations. This report, which engaged outsiders in discussion about its projects, including many NGOs, was intended to help create an environment of change in the organization. Although the central recommendation was for the Bank to create partnerships with borrower governments to engender project owner ship on the part of the borrower, the report also noted that participation of beneficiaries was important for project quality. The current Bank experimentation with participation of the poor was noted, and President Preston was quoted as saying he wanted participation to become the norm for the organization's operations in the future (World Bank, 1993). Although follow-up was undertaken in subsequent years, the Bank did not make serious efforts to improve project results until 1998.

NGOs continued to provide political support for the efforts of the Learning Group during the four years of its existence. Since the Learning Group's work represented the groundwork for a potential breakthrough in the Bank's approach to development, NGOs were enthusiastic about the initiative and monitored its progress.

Primarily through the avenue of the Working Group, NGOs prodded the Bank to take a bold approach to participation of the poor. As is evident in the chronology given in this chapter, at key points during the four-year learning period, the Working Group and other NGOs repeatedly emphasized three important points regarding participation. These were:

1   to keep a focus on the poor as the primary, most important stakeholders;
2   to take a transformational or demand-driven approach to participation; and
3   to make the key organizational changes necessary – in incentives and rewards, training, and procedural alterations – to enable incorporation of participatory processes into the Bank's operations.

As *The World Bank and Participation* (World Bank, 1994b) reveals, the organization embraced a portion of these NGO recommendations. First, the report pays attention, but not paramount attention, to the poor as the Bank's primary stakeholders. Second, although the report describes both instrumental as well as transformational participation, the organization embraces only the former as its approach to participation of the poor. The report describes the approach of several bilateral donors as focused on participation as an end as well as a means. These bilaterals, the Canadian International Development Authority (CIDA), GTZ, ODA – now called DFID — Sida, and USAID 'generally link their commitment to participation with their efforts in democratization, equity, good governance and human rights' (World Bank, 1994b). However, the Bank embraces only instrumental participation because it is explicitly prohibited from becoming involved in a country's political affairs by its Articles of

Agreement, and views transformational participation as political. Third, in the report, the Bank acknowledges the importance of organizational changes that would enable widespread incorporation of participation into its operations and commits itself to instituting some of these changes (incentives and rewards, selective recruitment, training, and revision of procurement guidelines).

Policy Implementation

Once the Board approved the Bank's report in September 1994, the implementation period for the action plan began. Armed with what was widely acknowledged as an excellent report and policy statement, it was now incumbent on the organization to translate its rhetoric into action.

World Bank Participation Initiatives

For several months there was a perceptible lull in energy regarding this work. The report had called for regional participation action plans to be prepared to incorporate participatory practices into Bank work. These were slow in coming. Finally, the senior oversight committee, formed to oversee implementation of the action plan, scheduled a meeting for April 1995 in order to spur the regions to draw up these plans and also called for regional participation coordinators to be named.

At the April 1995 meeting, the committee reviewed the draft regional participation action plans whose quality was uneven at best. The committee gave feedback and made requests for further information to each of the regions. Spurred on by skilful monitoring and assistance provided by the Participation Coordinator, the second drafts of these plans were a great improvement. Progress on implementation of these plans, however, varied considerably over the next two years and depended significantly on the interest of particular individuals. Lack of progress was also due partly to the fact that the April session of the oversight committee proved to be its one and only meeting, although it was mandated in the participation report to exist for two years. Without senior management oversight, attention to the regional action plans flagged. Ultimately, they were eclipsed by a new Bank effort to create social action plans. These plans were designed to include a variety of social issues and the specific focus on participation of the poor was lost.

Another effort to focus attention on participation of the poor began in late 1995, when 19 projects and policy development processes were designated as 'presidential flagships'. Quarterly reports on progress regarding participation in these initiatives were to be made directly to the Bank's president. These were intended to put a high profile on the need for participation in Bank work and were to be used to help its staff learn how to incorporate participatory practices into their work.

About a year later, reports on these 'flagships' were discontinued. Bank staff decided that these reports were not producing sufficient useful information, and that what its personnel needed were multiple sources of learning.

Another resource available to assist with participation efforts was the Fund for Innovative Approaches in Human and Social Development (FIAHS, or the Fund), established in July 1994. This fund, which provided over US$4 million during the subsequent three years,[9] was to be used to improve the quality of Bank operations in areas that had yet to be systematically incorporated into its operational work – specifically to promote participation – and in so doing to involve community-based organizations and NGOs and to undertake social assessments. It was available to both regional and central vice-presidencies and could be used for either operational or internal capacity building purposes. The Fund was intended as a supplement, not a substitute for regular departmental budgets. Indeed, a requirement was that all allocations had to be matched on a 50/50 basis with regular budget funds. The primary rationale for the Fund arose from growing evidence that uneven financial and technical support were major disincentives for task managers who wanted to broaden stakeholder involvement or improve social analysis. It was also intended to encourage innovation. The Fund proved to be very popular, and was tapped widely by staff interested in using participatory methods (World Bank, 1994a).

Here again, however, the Fund was discontinued when the Bank's Strategic Compact was adopted in early 1997. The Strategic Compact was a major reorganization of the Bank designed to 'lower the institution's costs, raise productivity, and improve the quality of the projects and programs it supports' (World Bank, 1997b). The intention of the compact regarding participation was that regular budget resources would be used for these efforts. According to knowledgeable Bank staff, however, designation of funds for participation of the poor was dependent on interested task managers or division heads: the Strategic Compact did not serve as a bucket into which to dip for participation resources'.

Yet another effort to promote participation was the creation in 1995 of the Inter-Agency Group on Participation (IGP). Mandated by the *The World Bank and Participation* (World Bank, 1994b), this group was an inter-agency consultative learning group on participation designed to bring the Bank together with other institutions (donors, NGOs, and research and training institutes) to promote inter-organizational collaboration in the areas of learning, capacity building and dissemination of research results.

The Bank hosted two meetings of the IGP in 1995 at which significant momentum was gathered for joint actions. Two major complementary initiatives were discussed that were intended to encourage in-country learning processes that would rely on collaboration among national governments, civil society organizations and international organizations' country offices.

The first was the Participatory Action Learning Program (PAL), developed by the World Bank, its Economic Development Institute (EDI) and USAID. The programme was put before the IGP for sponsorship with the idea that such support would help to identify funding needed to carry it out. It was designed to produce joint action and learning by all partners (government, civil society and donor organizations), with documentation and dissemination of experiences. The emphasis was to be on enabling poor and marginalized groups to have a voice in the development process. Objectives included demonstration of how donors could play a supportive role in national capacity building; creation of a common vision and support for participatory development; methodological learning and action about participation; strengthened capacity for participatory research and training; and evaluation, documentation and dissemination of lessons learned (Tandon, 1996b).

The second was the Learning and Action to Mainstream Participation (LAMP), developed by the EDI. This was a Bank-funded initiative and was presented to the IGP with the hope that the members of the group would become involved.

It was intended to establish and strengthen partnerships among government, civil society and donors; to structure action concurrently with learning by all partners; and to include the poor and marginalized by promoting practical approaches that effectively enable their voices to be heard in the design and implementation processes of development assistance programmes. Key tasks in the programme were to be information management services through documentation and dissemination of participatory experiences and practice; preparation of innovative participatory products such as tools, guidelines and frameworks; programme monitoring and evaluation; and 'just-in-time' joint training and learning in-country to respond to joint demands from both donor programme designers and local practitioners for assistance to launch new policy, sector or project initiatives in a participatory way (Tandon, 1996b).

In spite of this promising beginning, momentum was lost when the third meeting of the IGP was held in September 1996. The sponsorship of the IGP was intended to be shared among its members. After the World Bank had hosted the first two meetings, the UNDP took responsibility for the third. Participants at that meeting recalled that the format was that of an academic seminar focused on topics of interest to UNDP, with little or no effort to relate the meeting's agenda to the earlier two meetings. Neither of the initiatives nor a synthesis paper on generic lessons learned about participation that could have been valuable to all IGP participants (CIDA, 1997) were discussed: interest declined and the opportunity that the IGP represented in its early days faded away.

One LAMP programme was piloted in Sierra Leone and was very successful in launching an initiative that continues today. The division of EDI in which it had been developed, however, changed its priorities shortly after this first pilot programme, and the programme ended.

During the period 1995–1998, two major reference works were prepared by Bank staff. The first was the *Participation Sourcebook*, published in February 1996 and launched at a high-profile event described later in this chapter. It was designed as a resource on participatory methods and new ways of working to be used by those 'who have already decided to use participatory approaches in their professional work' (World Bank, 1996a). The second was *Participatory Tools and Techniques: A Resource Kit for Participation and Social Assessment*, published originally in 1997, with a revised and updated version called *Participation and Social Assessment: Tools and Techniques* (Rietbergen-McCracken and Narayan, 1998). This resource kit was prepared 'in order to support the adoption of participatory approaches in World Bank-supported projects and studies'. It contained a video as well as a lengthy reference document, replete with essential information about different methods and applications providing practical guidance and case examples.

The Influence of the new President on Participation

In June 1995, James D Wolfensohn took over the reins of the Bank as president and demonstrated that he was prepared to lead it towards a different style of operations. He urged the Bank, NGOs and all participants in development to work together more harmoniously given the common agenda of poverty reduction that all shared. He described effective development as evidenced by 'the smile on a child's face'. By his leadership and human touch, he began to destroy the stereotype of elite intellectualism and remote economics that many felt were hallmarks of the Bank, and within six months of his arrival, had taken several important steps that, directly or indirectly, helped promote participation of the poor.

- Nineteen projects and policies under development were designated as 'presidential flagships': quarterly reports to the president would ascertain whether effective participation of the poor was being incorporated in their design and implementation.
- At the recommendation of the Working Group, in late 1995, the position of NGO liaison officer was created in Bank resident missions to facilitate the organization's outreach to NGOs and other civil society organizations and, ideally, to create partnerships among the government, civil society and the Bank as envisioned in the IGP initiatives. At present, there are 70 NGO liaison officers out of a total of 90 resident Bank missions – in a few instances, one officer is responsible for more than one country.
- At meetings with US-based NGOs arranged by the president, NGO representatives requested that the Bank engage with borrower governments and civil society organizations in specific countries in a joint review of structural adjustment programmes. This resulted in the Structural Adjustment Participatory Review Initiative (SAPRI) which was formally launched in July 1997 and is currently being carried out jointly in eight countries and by civil society organizations alone in Mexico and the Philippines. Recently, work on development of alternative policies has been initiated in a number of these countries and in others as well. SAPRI was the first successful effort by NGOs to have the Bank acknowledge the need to include the poor in reviews of structural adjustment policies.
- In February 1996, the president made the opening speech at the launching ceremony of the *Participation Sourcebook* (World Bank, 1996a). The launch, held at Bank headquarters in Washington, DC, had a live video hook-up to a regional meeting of the Working Group in Accra, Ghana. In his speech, the president expressed surprise that such a meeting and resource were necessary and that participation of the poor was not already an integral part of the Bank's work. He noted that involvement of affected people in planning and design of initiatives intended to help them was such a commonsense notion that he was amazed it hadn't become part of Bank operations long ago.

Constraints to Policy Implementation

Of the several Bank participation of the poor initiatives begun at headquarters in 1995 and 1996 described above, none survived more than one or two years at most. These results reveal both the ad hoc nature of Bank efforts and an obvious lack of determination to implement the action plan included in the 1994 *World Bank and Participation* report. Indeed, the 1994 report did not trigger the development of an operational policy, which is the normal policy instrument used at the Bank.

Another organizational issue that has continued to hinder efforts at participation is the pressure on staff to move money – that is, to formulate, prepare and bring loan proposals before the Bank's board for approval – and to get money disbursed to borrowers (see Incentives and Rewards in Chapter 4). Although there have been changes in the personnel evaluation system that now reward teamwork and a client orientation, nothing has been done to reward participatory work and to relieve staff from the urgency to move money.

A related constraint has continued to be the use of the Bank's project cycle. Although learning innovation loans and adaptable lending instruments were introduced in 1997 (see Chapter 4) they have been used on a relatively small scale and do not directly provide for participation of the poor. No serious rethinking of the project cycle has been undertaken. The inflexibility of the project cycle phases remains, meaning that it is extremely difficult to incorporate participation of the poor in the formulation and design phases.

Another indication of a lack of serious interest in participation of the poor at headquarters was evident in the fact that after Aubrey Williams, Participation Coordinator since 1990, left his post in 1997 to assume a new job in the Bank, the position remained vacant for approximately a year and a half. It was finally filled in October 1998. NGO activists who were deeply involved in promoting participation during these years found that keeping the World Bank's attention was very hard.

The Strategic Compact has had an effect on participation efforts as well. Launched in early 1997, this was an agency-wide programme to reorganize and renew the Bank by improving its services to client countries, to carry forward a more complex development agenda and to revamp its capacity to deliver results (World Bank, 1997b). The Strategic Compact brought with it a net additional investment – excluding the cost of staff separations – of US$250 million, some of which was provided through a stringent programme of savings and redeployment. By financial year 2001, the administrative budget was to return to the 1997 level in real terms, subject to demand for the

Bank's improved products and services (World Bank, 1998). Some staff felt that this generally positive effort, which began devolving decision-making authority to the country level, drew attention away from participation of the poor and subsumed it under a more general category called Social Development. The adoption of the Strategic Compact also meant elimination of the FIAHS, which had directly funded participation work. Under the Strategic Compact, funds for participation were allocated by country department heads, thus making funding dependent on the commitment of the particular decision-maker to participation.

The Strategic Compact was a 30-month programme and came to an end on 30 June 2000: its completion put participation of the poor as well as the entire social and environmental agendas at risk. Most of the money for social assessments, which had made a lot of participation possible, disappeared. Given intense debates in the face of such a significant budget reduction, participation and social assessments were vulnerable to being sacrificed, particularly since they were optional as opposed to required policies.

It is only fair to note that significant efforts to promote participation – albeit on a largely ad hoc basis – went on during these years at project and policy levels in borrower countries in spite of the failures to mainstream participation. No reliable evaluation statistics on the extent of participation in project cycle phases or policy formulation processes were to be available until after a Bank-wide participation process review was completed in 2000. Based on more limited Bank investigation, however, data show that at least for socially oriented projects, involvement of the poor in project planning and implementation is now more extensive, although still very limited in project formulation and extremely low in evaluation phases (Narayan and Kochar, nd).

Working Group Involvement in the Implementation Phase

Encouraged by the September 1994 adoption of *The World Bank and Participation*, the Working Group re-activated the subgroup on participation of the poor in 1995 and committed itself to a two-year workplan with two purposes. These were to monitor and influence effective implementation of the World Bank policy on participation, and to promote wider and deeper involvement of civil society participants (development NGOs in particular) in the World Bank's participatory development efforts. The key elements of the subgroup's initial strategy were to:

1   focus on the Bank's regional participation action plans over a two-year time frame;

2   promote continuous and sustained information dissemination among civil society participants at regional and local levels and facilitate engagement with such processes;
3   influence headquarters, regional and country departments of the World Bank to improve both policy and project design, implementation and monitoring of participation; and
4   promote capacity building of civil society organizations, government agencies and World Bank staff to foster deeper and more sustained efforts in promoting local stakeholder participation (Tandon, 1995).

The subgroup intended to prepare a report on results of this work by mid-1997 in order to feed into a Bank review of participation efforts planned for that time.

An important change in the modus operandi of the Working Group took place at the time the subgroup on participation was determining its workplan: it began to decentralize its work. Traditionally, the Working Group had met twice a year, once in March when the NGO–World Bank Committee's Steering Committee met and once in October, when the full NGO–World Bank Committee met. The March meeting normally took place in a Southern country's capital although the agenda had a global rather than a regional focus. The October meeting always took place at the Bank's headquarters in Washington, DC. In 1995, the Working Group began to hold an annual regional meeting in each of the three Southern regions of Asia, Africa and Latin America, and continued to hold one annual meeting at Bank headquarters in October. The decentralized meetings, held each year in a different country of the particular region, enabled a more narrow geographic focus and gave many more Southern NGOs the opportunity to participate in their region, to learn about the Bank and its activities in their countries, and to become advocates for issues of greatest concern to them.

As these regional meetings began, the Working Group pressed for a commitment to have the relevant geographic vice-president attend the NGO–World Bank Committee meeting in his region. In the cases of Latin America and Africa, vice-presidents agreed and began attending each year. The same was not the case for Asia, however. As of 1998, vice presidents for South Asia and East Asia and the Pacific had not attended a single one of the four regional meetings held since 1995, despite repeated requests from the Working Group. In all regions, other senior regional Bank staff began to attend these meetings.

Approximately 30 or more NGOs from countries in the region attended the first of each regional meeting of the Working Group.

The number of NGOs has continued to grow with each year and over 85 NGOs attended the June 1998 Asia Pacific regional meeting.

A key part of the subgroup's workplan was the dissemination of Bank information regarding participation to NGOs in Southern countries. Working Group members translated essential Bank documents on participation, specific projects and policies into local languages and distributed them as widely as possible in their regions. Working Group members and other NGOs also continued urging the Bank to make information available in local languages.

A major part of the Working Group subgroup's approach was to monitor Bank projects at the country level and use such information to have face-to-face discussions with the Bank at headquarters, regional and country levels. The intention was that this dialogue based on actual Bank projects would lead to greater understanding and collaboration between the organization, NGOs and governments, as well as the opportunity to build greater capacity in participation of the poor for all participants, including the poor. Starting in March 1995 and continuing in every regional and global meeting held through 1998, discussions took place on participation in Bank project and policy work, usually through case studies prepared by NGOs.

Several of the cases monitored by the Working Group were funded through the IDA. In their analysis, the Group called for improved performance by the Bank and continued to support IDA funding. In 1995 and 1996, both Asian and African NGOs at regional Working Group meetings wrote statements supporting full funding for the IDA while calling for Bank reforms. These statements were shared with IDA deputies and sometimes with the US Congress and European governments as they deliberated on IDA replenishment.

Since 1994, IDA replenishment has become increasingly difficult, given the decline of overseas development assistance and increasingly isolationist tendencies within some parliaments and the US Congress. Therefore, support for the IDA by the Working Group was very important to the Bank, especially in the light of continuing calls for cuts by environmental and other NGOs. The NGO co-chair of the NGO–Bank Committee at the time, Manuel Chiriboga, wrote in an analysis of the Working Group, 'This Working Group position, which was followed up with pro-active campaigning with donor countries, gave the group leverage power [regarding participation and other important topics] with the Bank, which it lacked up to then' (Chiriboga M, 1999).

In October 1995, at the time of the global meeting of the NGO–World Bank Committee, the NGOs learned in a session with the president about the designation of 'presidential flagships', noted earlier in this chapter. Given the high visibility these initiatives were sure to have inside the Bank, and therefore the potential for using them to influence change, the Working Group subgroup on participation decided to monitor a certain number of these flagships.

During the next year, in addition to continuing its work on monitoring participation in projects, the Working Group began to focus attention on participation in formulation of Bank policies, with particular attention to the Bank's Country Assistance Strategy (CAS). For example, it was at the regional meeting in Nicaragua in March 1996 that the Bank's vice-president for Latin America, Javed Burki, accepted a request from the Working Group to formulate two to three CASs in a participatory way. Subsequently, development of the assistance strategy in El Salvador, Colombia and Peru was undertaken including participation of civil society organizations.

A key aspect of the Working Group's strategy to influence the Bank on participation of the poor and other key issues was making the board of directors of the World Bank an advocacy target. Its meeting with the Bank's Board in October 1996 was the first time a group of NGOs had met with the entire group of Bank executive directors. Meetings in subsequent years have become true exchanges of views, with spirited discussion taking place about participation and other issues of importance.

At the October 1996 global meeting of the NGO–World Bank Committee, the Working Group participation subgroup announced an adaptation of its strategy, based on its assessment of what the Bank had done in the preceding year and a half (Tandon, 1996a). Several important issues were identified through the work of the subgroup's monitoring of Bank projects that needed attention. These included:

- an almost total lack of timely information in local languages regarding Bank projects;
- a variety of problems associated with participation of the poor in Bank projects (virtually no involvement in formulation and design; no continuity of key participants such as NGOs over stages of the project cycle; no shared decision-making with the poor regarding resources earmarked for a project; no capacity building efforts for the poor, nor any resources to enable them to participate effectively in Bank projects;
- virtually no participation by the poor or NGOs in Bank policy formulation; and
- very little effort by the Bank on reform of borrower government institutions, resulting in formidable constraints to participation of the poor .

Both the promising initiatives the Bank had started as well as these disturbing findings led the subgroup to present an action plan for the years 1997 and 1998 that focused on intensified *and* broadened efforts. In part, the subgroup would focus more on the Bank's own participation initiatives – especially the 'flagships' and the IGP – to make progress. The subgroup's 1995 workplan had generally targeted its monitoring towards the Bank's overall participation action plan and promotion of wider and deeper involvement of development NGOs in the Bank's participatory development efforts. The 1997–1998 action plan had two significant changes: a specific focus on participation by the poor and attention to projects supported not only by the Bank but also by other multilateral, bilateral and borrower government agencies. Specific steps to be taken to carry out the new action plan were:

- evolution of a common framework for participation of the poor;
- launch of an 18-month monitoring process of Bank projects and policies in the three regions of Africa, Asia and Latin America, using the common framework;
- capacity building of extended partner NGO networks engaged in the monitoring process;
- formation of in-country learning groups (as outlined in the PAL initiative emanating from the IGP) to increase capacity of NGOs, international donor agencies and borrower/recipient governments in participation; and
- a global seminar in 1998 to synthesize and share lessons learned (Tandon, 1996b).

The subgroup launched this ambitious effort with a training workshop on monitoring of participation in World Bank programmes in February 1997 in Addis Ababa, Ethiopia. Sixteen NGO representatives from Africa, Asia and Latin America attended. Participants agreed on a common monitoring framework and the criteria for selection of specific projects and policies to monitor. Monitoring of several projects had been started earlier by subgroup members and further investigation of these would continue as part of the overall effort. All agreed to share findings with implementing government agencies, as well as with the Bank in subsequent regional NGO–Bank committee meetings prior to publishing any results. Findings would be presented at the global seminar anticipated to occur in mid-1998 prior to the Bank's own review of its participation efforts.

Despite extremely limited financial and human resources, NGOs in the three regions carried out this monitoring effort during the ensuing 18 months. Initially, NGOs had hoped that the Bank and the respective recipient government implementing agencies would participate in the monitoring. This was actively explored in all cases, but agreement was reached in only a few instances. Ultimately, NGOs produced reports on nine Bank projects and nine CAS processes from the three regions. Although some of these were of uneven quality, they did enable the Working Group to engage the Bank in a systematic way regarding progress on participation of the poor and were a key factor in the Working Group's success in holding the 1998 Participation Conference.

In addition to this monitoring effort, the Working Group sought to fill the void left by the failure of the IGP. The first two meetings of the IGP had revealed two areas for potential collaboration among multilateral and bilateral donors and NGOs. These were the need to build capacity for participation work at country level in government implementing agencies and civil society; and organizational reform in large donor agencies in order to enable participation of the poor (Participation Subgroup, 1998).

Motivated partly by the early discussions in the IGP, several bilateral donors had begun to synthesize their experiences in participation of the poor with a view to improving their policies and programmes. In late 1997, the Working Group began negotiating directly with these donors and the Bank to hold a multi-stakeholder conference in 1998 focused on participation of the poor. At the invitation of the Working Group, the IDS agreed to become a co-sponsor of the conference. By early 1998, the bank president had committed the Bank to be a co-sponsor. The Working Group then invited several bilateral donors to become sponsors and collaborate in the design of the conference. Four bilateral donors – DFID, GTZ, Sida and USAID – agreed to join the effort.

The conference preparatory committee, comprised of a representative from each sponsoring agency, met for a workshop in England in July 1998 where they synthesized lessons from the NGO monitoring studies of World Bank projects and policies, discussed participation experiences in other donor agencies and planned the conference.

On 19 and 20 November 1998, the conference was held at World Bank headquarters in Washington, DC. Entitled *The International Conference on Upscaling and Mainstreaming Participation of Primary Stakeholders: Lessons Learned and Ways Forward*, it was attended by representatives of all sponsoring agencies, other donors, Southern and Northern NGOs, Southern government officials, and researchers. It was the first time that such a diverse group had come together to share lessons regarding participation of the poor in large-scale development projects and policy formulation. It served as a stocktaking on the decade of effort by all these donors and NGOs to promote participation of the poor and was the impetus for this book.

Convergence Among NGOs on a Call for Participation in Bank Policy Formulation

As noted earlier, beginning in 1995, Working Group members increased their calls for participation in policy development processes. Initially, the Learning Group had focused only on participation in Bank-financed projects. However, NGOs noted that unless civil society representatives or the poor, themselves, were involved in formulation of development policies, the national and sectoral frameworks for Bank-financed work in a country would be determined before the views of the poor and marginalized were ever sought for particular projects.

NGOs called especially for participation in country assistance strategies and in development of policy papers which the Bank calls Economic and Sector Work (ESW). These included poverty assessments, public expenditure reviews and specific sectoral policy papers. These papers are considered by the Bank as 'building blocks' to be used to help prepare the CAS (although many inside the Bank admit that they are often not used). The Working Group also began urging the Bank to make the draft CAS available to civil society representatives invited to consult on preparation of this paper. (See particular recommendations regarding participation in CAS formulation in Chapter 3.)

SAPRI, with its emphasis on participation of the poor in the Bank's economic policy formulation, was proposed in 1995 and launched in 1997. Between 1995 and 1998, many NGOs around the world began calling for civil society participation in the formulation of country assistance strategies and other important Bank policies, and for their publication. In fact, these became advocacy issues 'in common' among NGOs regardless of whatever other issues they were advocating with the Bank.

Related NGO Campaigns that Supported Participation of the Poor

Although the Working Group had participation as a central advocacy issue, other NGO campaigns supported participation as well. Some of the major efforts are included here.

Disclosure

Access to information was the first issue for which NGOs lobbied the Bank in the early 1980s, and advocacy for full disclosure continues until the present day. It is the basic precondition for all forms of participation. Begun by two lawyers based in Washington, DC in 1983, the information disclosure effort has been led by the Bank Information Center (BIC) since 1987. BIC is a non-profit information service for NGOs in Southern countries that also monitors the social and environmental impacts of multilateral development bank lending. In the early days, the desire for information was specifically related to Bank design and implementation of large infrastructure projects with actual or potential negative environmental effects. In the case of dams, a related issue was resettlement of mainly poor people who were largely uninformed by either the Bank or their government as to the projects or their terms.

During the first decade of advocacy on this topic, Bank documents were often 'leaked' to NGOs by staff interested in supporting reforms. Finally, in 1993, following the campaign to stop the Narmada Dam in India, NGOs used the funding authority of Northern donor governments of IDA to force the Bank into revising its information policy in favour of disclosure (see Background earlier in this chapter). The revised policy created a project information document, written by a project's task manager very early in the project cycle to be updated as the project moves forward, although according to BIC this is rarely done (BIC, 1999): it can be provided to the public upon request. A second element allows release of 'factual technical information' about a project (feasibility studies, technical studies and poverty analyses for example) before loan approval.

Since this first partial victory, NGOs have continued to press for greater access. They have advocated translation of Bank documents into local languages and dissemination to the poor and intermediary organizations involved in project development and in consultations regarding country assistance strategies. Many NGOs have advocated publication of the country assistance strategies.

Philosophically, some senior Bank managers are in favour of greater disclosure. Gloria Davis, Director of the Social Development Department until 2000, gave evidence of this in her presentation to the 1998 participation conference. She urged those present to create an even stronger demand for information in the Bank's client countries. Moreover, at that same meeting, President Wolfensohn said, in relation to the Bank's new Comprehensive Development Framework (CDF): 'We will have absolute disclosure of our experience in this exercise, because in these cases we'll have the governments with us and we'll tell them that we're going to fully disclose what happens' (Wolfensohn, 1998). In spite of these encouraging statements, Bank current practice lags far behind. In December 1999, BIC, in commenting on a Bank issues paper on information disclosure, noted:

> *In 1999 the World Bank has announced two major initiatives predicated upon participation and inclusiveness ... the Comprehensive Development Framework and the Poverty Reduction Strategy Paper ... The draft of the Information Disclosure Issues Paper does not reflect the new spirit of participation and has overlooked the importance of information disclosure to the new development paradigm ... As long as documents such as draft project appraisal documents and draft Country Assistance Strategies remain confidential, the Bank's stated commitment to participation will ring hollow to those who are affected by, or could contribute to, a given loan* (BIC, 1999)

A recent violation of the Bank's policy occurred in the China Western Poverty Reduction Project. This controversial project was cancelled on 7 July 2000 following a scathing inspection panel report; widespread media coverage including several editorials calling for the project's cancellation; pressure from the US Congress and parliamentarians in other countries, and Tibetans kneeling in front of the door to Bank headquarters with their mouths gagged holding a sign that read 'Social Assessment'. The panel report observed that there existed a 'climate of fear' in the project area which would make any meaningful consultation with project-affected people impossible. Informed consultation is a prerequisite to the Indigenous Peoples, Resettlement and Environmental Assessment policies.[10]

Inspection Panel
Successful NGO efforts in the early 1990s, which convinced the Bank to create an inspection panel, and continued advocacy to improve the panel since its establishment in 1994, have reinforced another fundamental aspect of participation – accountability to citizens for results of projects or for their adverse effects. The impetus for this panel came from negative effects of large infrastructure projects funded by the Bank. Early NGO reform efforts focused on Bank policies and procedures related to large infrastructure projects. NGOs soon realized, however, that even with reform policies in place, there were no systematic internal rules within the Bank for ensuring that staff consistently follow these reform policies (Fox and Brown, 1998).

In the same NGO campaign that resulted in a revised Bank information disclosure policy, environmental activists used the funding authority of Northern donor governments to force the Bank to create an inspection panel (see Background earlier in this chapter). Seven years after its establishment, two claims filed with the panel have contributed to cancellation of projects: the Arun III dam in Nepal in 1995 and the China Western Poverty Reduction Project in 2000. Weaknesses in the panel persist regarding public access, its independence, limited information disclosure during the inspection process, the fact that it cannot accept claims for projects for which the loan money has been substantially disbursed, and its limited jurisdiction to only two of the four institutions in the World Bank Group (Udall, 1998).

Although the establishment of an inspection panel was a major step forward in terms of the Bank's accountability to citizens of borrower countries, it is clear from the ways in which it has tried to limit its scope and functioning since then that full accountability is far from assured. Following continued NGO advocacy, on 20 April 1999, the Bank's board approved a report of the Working Group on the second review of the inspection panel. The report's conclusions were intended to strengthen and enhance the role of the inspection panel. The review included consultations with NGOs and other civil society organizations after the report was first circulated which resulted in revisions to the report (World Bank, 1999).

Structural Adjustment Participatory Review Initiative

As described earlier, SAPRI was proposed by NGOs in June 1995 and, following a long period of negotiation, was launched at Bank headquarters in Washington, DC in July 1997.

The heart of this initiative is a call for participation of civil society and the poor in the development of economic policies intended for their countries. The review has been designed to have representatives from civil society, together with Bank and national government representatives, jointly assess the impact of structural adjustment in the country. Based on this review, the three parties are to make recommendations for how economic policies should be formulated in the future.

Each review began with mobilization of civil society and the convening of regional workshops and meetings in preparation for an opening national forum in each country. At the forum, a diverse cross-section of civil society organizations conveyed its assessment of the impact of adjustment policies on the country. In addition, the opening forum helped to set the agenda for participatory field research. Such research has been completed in two countries and is anticipated to be finished in all countries in 2001. In 2001, a second national forum is to be held in each country, at which the findings from the first forum and the research will be presented and assessed. The process will culminate in a global conference in 2001 at Bank headquarters in Washington, DC. This initiative, as well as support to the SAPRI network of civil society organizations around the world is coordinated by the Development Group for Alternative Policies (D'GAP), a US NGO, from their office in Washington, DC (Hellinger, 2000).

Campaign for Gender Integration

Gender advocates can rightly argue that their efforts are central to the promotion of the participation of the poor, since poor women are among the most marginalized in any population and are routinely ignored by development planners ... even 'participatory' development planners.

Although women's organizations and other NGOs had advocated for greater attention to gender concerns for many years with some success, such efforts intensified at the time of the 1995 Fourth World Women's Conference in Beijing, China. At Beijing, President Wolfensohn made a speech regarding the institution's attention to gender issues. There, he was presented with a statement, signed by 900 women from around the world, calling for integration of women into the work of the Bank. Promoting the participation of women at the grassroots in economic policy formulation was one of four main challenges made to the Bank (Williams, 1997).

This was the beginning of a global advocacy effort on gender called 'Women's Eyes on the [World] Bank' campaign, which continues to the present day. In 1997, the campaign published a review of gender integration in World Bank policy and practice entitled *Gender Equity and the World Bank Group: A Post-Beijing Assessment* (Williams, 1997). Throughout its work, the campaign has continued to call for inclusion of women in the promotion of participation. Like the participation efforts of NGOs, advocacy on gender has been carried out through an 'inside/outside' strategy, with NGOs, academics and other gender advocates outside the Bank aligning with gender activists inside it.

Implementation Monitoring

InterAction, a consortium of 155 US NGOs, headquartered in Washington, DC, and its members, most especially Bread for the World Institute's Development Bank Watchers' Project, have advocated participation of the poor since the days of the Learning Group.[11] The project's director at the time played a key role in drafting the NGO addendum to the Bank's 1994 *World Bank and Participation* report. In February 1997, InterAction proposed that the

Bank mandate participation in project and policy development processes. At least partly as a result of this proposal, the Bank revised its project concept document (required to be completed by task team leaders during the project identification phase) to incorporate specific questions – some actually written by the Development Bank Watchers' Project director – about participation undertaken and intended for the remainder of the project.

In mid-1998, InterAction analysed findings from the first new project concept document. Although done on a small sample, the report's conclusions are the same as those reported in this book regarding the limited extent of the participation of the poor in the identification phase of projects and the level of participation in the Bank (InterAction, 1999).

INITIATIVE RESULTS AND NGO CONTRIBUTIONS

The Bank's own data on levels of participation of the poor in phases of the project cycle is limited at best (see Chapter 3 for more details on monitoring efforts). As far as can be determined, such participation occurs only a tenth of the time in the earliest and, in many respects, most important formulation phase, and perhaps a third of the time in the design phase. In implementation, close to half of projects involve the poor, while their involvement in evaluation is lowest of all, at less than 10 per cent. Bank efforts to involve civil society and the poor in policy formulation processes began in earnest about four years ago. Some progress has been made thus far, with considerably more work to be done. Certain assessments regarding the degree of progress can be made with some confidence:

1   The Bank's environment is now more receptive to new ideas. The Learning Group, together with the Wapenhans Report, the Strategic Compact, and the executive training that has gone on for the past two years, in addition to the president's leadership, have changed the atmosphere in the agency.
2   There has been a noticeable shift in attitude of many staff away from seeing themselves as 'experts' to understanding the need to see each project or policy development process in its own context, with its own cultural, economic, social and geographic variables.
3   The Bank, itself, in its report prepared for the 1998 November conference, acknowledges that participatory approaches are far from being general to the Bank's work. Some excellent participatory work has been done in various projects, although

participation in project formulation and in project evaluation remains very low. Achievements continue to be heavily dependent on the personal interests of staff and management involved rather than the result of organizational incentives and systems. In some regions, a great deal is happening, but there are increasing concerns about the *quality* of many participation activities.

4   Progress has been made in the participation of civil society representatives and the poor in policy development processes. Beginning with virtually no participation in 1994, a Bank study in 1999 showed that 40 per cent of CASs developed in 1999 and 2000 had a high level of participation (Shah and Tikare, 1999). This is an encouraging trend. A host of issues, however, including the quality of civil society participation, the way in which it was carried out, the timely availability of strategy-related information to those consulted, the resultant impact on the final strategy document, and appropriate Bank feedback to civil society all must be assessed before determining the value of such consultations (see Chapter 3 for an assessment of civil society participation in development of these strategies).

5   A second generation of work on participation of the poor has begun at the Bank. Plans include more intensive training, along with creation of small learning groups, alliances, and feedback circles to aid continuous learning. It is expected that quality standards for participation are to be developed and applied to the work of World Bank staff.

6   Another sign that the Bank is learning from the experiences of the past is the CDF, which was launched in a dozen countries during1999. This represents a significant opportunity for including participation in those countries' development processes. The CDF is to use a long-term and strategic approach where all the essential components of development are brought together. In the president's words, this development approach would 'be a participatory process, as transparent and as accountable as possible within the political climate prevailing in each country' (Wolfensohn, 1999).

7   A last encouraging sign relates to the 1999 adoption by the Bank of a poverty reduction strategy paper to replace the policy framework paper used previously to identify Bank and borrower government priorities, allocate resources and reassess strategies (World Bank, 1999). The new framework is an effort to implement the CDF 'in a way that would systematically link diagnosis and public actions to poverty outcomes' (World Bank, 1999a). In November 1999, guidelines for public consultation on the poverty strategy were prepared.

8   SAPRI is the only ongoing global effort related to participation of the poor that was proposed by NGOs and was *jointly* undertaken by the Bank, governments and civil society. Four years after its launch, the Bank has yet to establish a mechanism for integrating into its operations or policy-making activities what is being learned from national-level research and forums.

9   The Bank's organizational reforms, necessary in order to incorporate participation effectively into an agency, are analysed in detail in Chapter 4. These changes, which were called for during the Learning Group's life, in the 1994 report, and again at the November 1998 conference, for the most part have not been put in place.

In the course of the past ten years, NGOs around the world have been the major advocates for, and monitors of, the Bank's efforts to include participation of the poor in its operations. For the five years before the Bank became interested in participation, NGO environmental activists had lobbied vigorously about negative effects of Bank-financed projects on the environment and the poor, and the fact that no information was available to people affected by these projects. Some development NGOs, especially those in the Working Group at the time, had begun to call attention to the adverse effects of structural adjustment on the poor. It was largely because of the extent of environmental NGO activism vis-à-vis the institution that the Bank was motivated to hold its 1987 meeting with NGOs, at which participants agreed on the need for Bank collaboration with Southern NGOs. This meeting led directly to the establishment of an NGO unit within the Strategic Planning Division of the Bank.

Prior to 1995, members of the Working Group, with rare exceptions, were unable or unwilling to commit significant amounts of time to World Bank reform work between meetings. Two notable exceptions in the early days were D'GAP and Oxfam GB (known prior to 1998 as Oxfam UK and Ireland), each of which served two terms on the Group. It was largely due to the efforts of D'GAP that the 1987 consensus document and the 1989 position paper on the Bank were written. Later, in 1991 after the *Saly Declaration* was written, again it was D'GAP that raised funds and coordinated efforts to ensure that three case studies reviewing structural adjustment programmes in Sri Lanka, Senegal and Mexico were done. Oxfam UK and Ireland took a lead role in proposing a social audit of Bank projects as a way to determine effects of Bank-funded interventions on the poor. This approach was put forward during the Learning Group's work. Such a consistent investment of time and effort by Working Group members did not occur again until 1995.

Once the rejuvenated Working Group subgroup on participation of the poor carved out its workplan in 1995, a systematic NGO monitoring and promotion effort began. Unlike the earlier Working Group effort adopted in the 1991 *Saly Declaration*, which created two distinct and separate working groups on structural adjustment and participation, the later strategy linked participation with substantive policy issues. This was most notable in the efforts to incorporate civil society and the poor into formulation of the Bank's country assistance strategies and economic and sector work.

The three-year period from 1995 to 1998 saw the most consistent promotion of participation of the poor at any time since the topic was first introduced at the World Bank in 1987. The Working Group strategy, together with advocacy efforts of many other NGOs around the world, served to keep participation on the Bank's agenda during a period when the organization's interest in the topic waxed and waned.

A new and critically important aspect of the Working Group strategy adopted in 1995 was its focus not only on Bank headquarters but also on regional and country levels. The decision to regionalize its work and begin meeting once each year in each of the three regions of Asia, Africa, and Latin America and the Caribbean ensured that it was ready to engage with the Bank when it adopted the Strategic Compact in early 1997 – a happy 'unintended consequence'. The Strategic Compact called for more human and financial resources to be put on the 'front lines' of development, that is, at the country level. Significant numbers of staff who had been based at headquarters moved to borrower countries and began to engage more regularly with governments and civil society than had hitherto been the case.

The regional meetings of the Working Group also resulted in regular participation by the Latin America and Caribbean, and Africa vice-presidents. Once they started to attend meetings and became interested in the issues of the Working Group, task managers responsible for projects or policy formulation processes in countries of the region also became interested and started attending meetings. In addition, the Working Group monitoring of ongoing Bank projects and policy formulation processes in each region meant that it had an item of significant interest to regional Bank staff on the agenda of each meeting.

The combination of meetings in the regions and annual meetings at Bank headquarters helped the Working Group push its agenda on participation of the poor. Specific projects or country assistance strategies were discussed at regional levels, and then general lessons on the status of participation were drawn at the headquarters' meetings. The fact that the Working Group met regularly with the president, other senior staff at headquarters, and annually with the board, gave them standing with regional staff as well.

Through their efforts to promote participation at the Bank NGOs provided these essential things:

1   Political endorsement in the early days of the Learning Group when it had very little support inside the Bank.
2   Support to 'participation pioneers' inside the Bank who were struggling to promote and incorporate participatory processes in spite of the impediments posed by a lack of resources, the rigidities of the project cycle, time pressures, and demands to get projects approved quickly.
3   Alliances created with Bank staff who were developing ways to promote participation that resulted in pressure on the Bank to maintain and carry out its commitments.
4   An accountability mechanism for the Bank. The Working Group and other NGOs regularly reviewed progress on participation and repeatedly urged that the Bank adhere to its commitments made in *World Bank and Participation* (World Bank, 1994b).
5   Assurance that transparency regarding progress in incorporating participation would be maintained. NGOs were involved from the beginning of the participation effort and throughout the implementation phase of the action plan.
6   Regular engagement with the president to review progress.
7   Annual Working Group meetings since 1996 with the Bank's Board of Directors, which have begun to change the atmosphere in the Board towards NGOs and perhaps more generally towards the participation of the poor.

CONCLUSIONS AND LESSONS LEARNED

Lesson One

Both an organizational change strategy and a learning approach are essential to an organization's efforts to implement a major new policy. World Bank and Participation (World Bank, 1994b) serves as the Bank's policy on participation but the subsequent Bank efforts at its implementation have been half-hearted at best, and have not come close to reaching the goal of fully incorporating participation into its operations. One reason for this is that an organizational strategy was never developed to ensure implementation of the recommendations, so that efforts proceeded in an ad hoc way without the necessary political or management support. The other important reason is the approach taken by the Bank in each phase. Throughout the four years that the group existed, it learned, not only from work done by the Bank, itself, but perhaps more importantly, from a variety of outside organizations and individuals experienced in participation. The Bank's openness to listening to and absorbing information from others as to what is needed to carry out participatory development is reflected in the quality of the organization's 1994 report.

After adoption of the 1994 report, however, the Bank largely reverted to type. There was no strategy for implementation, and its ad hoc efforts at implementing the excellent set of recommendations relied mainly on its own staff. Where participation specialists from other organizations were involved in Bank projects and a more experimental process was used, results were better. Some of the projects that the Working Group monitored are examples of this. In Argentina, where it monitored a project on rural poverty, NGOs had several discussions with the relevant Argentine government units and the Bank's task manager responsible for the project. NGOs involved the poor in carrying out participatory evaluation during the project identification phase and strengthened a small NGO coalition to assist the project. Ultimately, the Argentine Rural Development Department wrote to the Working Group thanking them for the monitoring process and all they had learned from it about participation.

It must also be noted that the politics at work in particular recipient countries and the resulting stance of the Bank must be taken into account when considering the degree of success achieved in participation of the poor. Where countries were amenable to participation, Bank staff (at least those with an interest in participation) were able to make progress. According to Southern NGOs actively promoting participation, however, if a country's political culture was not open to participation, the organization simply adapted to that. The more general Bank failure in this regard has been the attitude of staff that it is the responsibility of the recipient government to incorporate participation into projects and policies, and that it is not the Bank staff's job to assist governments to learn how to do this.

Lesson Two

Constructive NGO advocacy can support internal efforts to reform by monitoring progress, challenging backsliding and rewarding success.

Since participation was first introduced at the Bank, the NGOs' greatest success has been in promoting and keeping participation of the poor on the organization's agenda. Had it not been for the support of

NGOs, the Learning Group might never have been formed, and it might not have survived. It is also true that while some progress has taken place in incorporating participation into Bank programmes, the overall effort might have fallen by the wayside at any point during the years since the 1994 report was adopted had it not been for the work of the Working Group and other NGOs around the world.

The Working Group was well situated to play the lead role in the effort to promote participation of the poor. First of all, it enjoyed a legitimacy in the eyes of the Bank that other NGOs did not necessarily have. This derived partly from the fact that it was the Bank that originally created the NGO–Bank Committee, and has continued to provide partial funding for its work. Even though the NGOs created the Working Group as early as 1984, and subsequently declared themselves advocates for reform, the Bank continued to accord them a special place. This may be due to two factors. The first is that by 1994 the vast majority of its members were from Southern NGOs, and the Bank has consistently stated a desire to work with NGOs *from* recipient countries. Secondly, the Working Group has always opted to engage in policy dialogue with the Bank rather than to use more confrontational tactics to pressure it to change, a technique that has been termed *critical cooperation* (Covey, 1998). Its behaviour regarding the IDA was an example of this. NGOs negotiated with the Bank and the IDA deputies regarding the need for participation and other reforms in Bank programmes while publicly supporting full funding of IDA. One could also say that the Working Group represented the moderate, non-threatening voice of reform vis-à-vis the Bank, whereas other NGOs – particularly those lobbying for environmental changes, information disclosure, the inspection panel, and an end to structural adjustment programmes – opted for more hard-line approaches, such as lobbying for legislation in the US Congress, which conditioned the IDA funding on Bank reforms, media campaigns, and demonstrations.[12]

From 1995 to 1998, the Working Group also benefited from the fact that James Wolfensohn was president of the Bank. He was a full supporter of participation and also wanted the Bank to be actively engaged with NGOs and other civil society organizations. His leadership and his frequent speeches in which he supported participation of the poor, one of the most important of which was his speech to the World Bank–IMF annual meeting in 1997 on the topic of inclusion, lent support to the participation effort.

Lastly, the leadership and advocacy skills of the members of the Working Group, particularly Steering Committee members during the years 1995 to 1998, enabled them to take advantage of opportunities to keep participation of the poor alive at the Bank. The ability of the Group to fill the void left by the failure of the IGP by calling for and succeeding in holding the 1998 Participation Conference is testimony to this fact. The conference forced the agency to take stock of, and make a public presentation on, the extent of progress it had achieved. It also reignited interest in participation of the poor at the Bank at a time when a new participation coordinator had just been hired. In effect, the conference provided him with a mandate to move forward vigorously. Lastly, by carrying out the conference in a multi-stakeholder way, the Working Group created a positive form of peer pressure among the five donor agencies involved regarding their actions to promote participation in their organizations.

In reflecting on the years between the Learning Group's participation report and the Participation Conference, Aubrey Williams, who served as the Bank's participation coordinator from 1991 to 1997, credited NGOs with ensuring that the Bank stayed focused on its commitment to participation.

> *Your [NGO] sustained commitment to the original plan of action [contained in the 1994 report] required that we regularly look at progress. It forced us to have OED do the evaluation of participation [completed in 2000]. The participation conference in November 1998, forced us to do focus groups and to write our report on progress. All that was very supportive of initiatives on the inside.* (Williams, 1998)

Lesson Three

Strong NGO capacities in research, analysis and advocacy, available subject matter expertise and sufficient financial resources are essential to be able to promote reform and influence change in large donor agencies.

Independent monitoring of Bank projects and policy formulation processes was the key to the results achieved by the Working Group effort on participation. Undertaking such an ambitious monitoring effort between 1995 and 1998 proved to be a very difficult task, however. Challenges faced in this monitoring experience helped Working Group members recognize the need to enhance their capacity to do research, policy analysis, advocacy and regional networking in order to be better equipped to influence policies of transnational bodies that had increasing impact at the country and local levels.

Although this research was intended to be done independently by NGOs, the Working Group had hoped to undertake the effort in cooperation with the Bank so that information could be shared and both sides could learn from the results. Bank staff at headquarters were very reluctant to become involved, however, maintaining that task managers (those responsible for specific projects) were already burdened by too much work. This lack of support from Bank headquarters meant that where its staff in recipient countries were uncooperative NGOs had to proceed on their own. This sometimes made getting the cooperation of recipient government implementing agencies harder or even impossible. In the cases where neither Bank nor government staff were involved, potential for joint learning among Bank, government and NGO staff through the monitoring work was lost.

In spite of these problems, doing global research together ultimately strengthened the Working Group, and created a framework for undertaking collective, inter-regional research. Having actual data on Bank projects and policies enabled the Working Group to engage regularly in dialogue with the Bank on the 'nuts and bolts' of actual project or policy development.

In a broader sense, the results the Working Group achieved between 1995 and 1998 were due to members' ability and willingness to commit time, resources and expertise to the effort. The fact that at least two of the member NGOs (the Society for Participatory Research in Asia [PRIA] from India, and the Institute for Development Research [IDR] from the United States) were organizations specializing in participation of the poor, and that certain other member NGOs and NGO networks had significant experience in participation, meant that the Working Group had sufficient expertise in the topic to have credibility with the Bank. Moreover, the ability of the Working Group to convince the IDS to co-sponsor the 1998 Participation Conference was essential to its success given the Institute's long involvement in researching and promoting primary stakeholder participation, as well as its prior involvement with the Bank on the topic.

Lesson Four

Southern and northern NGOs need to improve their ability to work together in coalitions in order to maximize impact.
Although the Working Group and other NGOs worked to promote participation of the poor in the World Bank, they did not work together closely enough to maximize their effectiveness. Although the

Working Group cooperated to some extent with InterAction, the Development Bank Watchers' Project and BIC, none of these efforts were discussed and negotiated early enough or fully enough to enable all sides to plot out a joint strategy that may have produced better results at the Bank. All three of the organizations mentioned are based in Washington, DC, where the Bank is headquartered. Both BIC and the Development Bank Watchers' Project are full-time information, monitoring and advocacy programmes focused on multilateral development bank reform. Although InterAction, as the major US NGO consortium, has a diversified programme, it had a major advocacy project focused on the World Bank. These organizations and the Working Group could have shared information with each other about their strategies and joined forces in a more deliberate way for greater impact.

Within the Working Group itself, the Northern NGO members played facilitative and supportive roles with Southern NGO representatives in the group. Given Northern NGOs' greater access to the Bank and their own donor institutions, and, in most cases if not all, their greater resources, these representatives could have sought leadership in their own right. Rather, they chose to support the Southern leadership within the Working Group and the effort beginning in 1995 to shift the focus of attention to Southern regions in order to expand outreach to Southern NGOs.

Efforts began in 1997 to restructure the Working Group to have five main regional assemblies, corresponding roughly to the Bank's five regions, with Northern NGO assemblies in North America, Europe, Australia and Japan, and a representative global steering committee. This undertaking was intended to create a coalition effort to produce NGO cohesion and strength within the regions for greater advocacy effect, and solidarity on common advocacy targets. This was, and continues to be, a complicated endeavour, dealing with different organizational mandates, pre-existing relationships and partnerships, regional differences, varying degrees of resources and personal orientations – issues with which the Working Group and the three Washington-based organizations mentioned above did not come to grips regarding advocacy on the promotion of participation. If the continued restructuring is successful, however, it could result in a much stronger, more unified and forceful NGO voice for World Bank reform.

Chapter 3

Participation in Development Initiatives

BACKGROUND

During the early years in which donor agencies undertook the practice of participation of the poor, their efforts were focused almost exclusively on projects and much was learned about the complexity of how to involve the poor in the formulation, design, planning, implementation and evaluation of projects. Since 1996, prompted by vigorous advocacy by NGOs around the world, these agencies have acknowledged that the poor should also participate in the formulation of development policies in their countries.

This chapter examines the experience of three large donor agencies' efforts to incorporate participation of the poor into projects and policy development processes. At the November 1998 Participation Conference, three of the international donor agencies co-sponsoring the conference shared their experiences in integrating participation into projects and policy formulation. The first was a presentation by the Working Group regarding a three-year monitoring process of World Bank-funded projects and policies. The second was by GTZ regarding their 12 years of experience in incorporating the participation of the poor into their development project work. The third was by the International NGO Training and Research Centre (INTRAC) and the DFID, Britain's foreign aid agency, regarding a study that examined the experience of DFID in incorporating participation into their development work in five countries. INTRAC is a British NGO that provides management training and research services for European NGOs and focuses on improving organizational effectiveness and programme performance of Northern NGOs and Southern partners. The organization was contracted by DFID as an independent evaluator to examine the work of DFID. Workshops in which participants examined aspects of participation, such as involvement of the poor in projects and policy development processes, capacity building and participatory monitoring and evaluation also took place at the conference.

PARTICIPATION IN PROJECTS

Poor people know best their own economic and social needs and problems, and have insights and ideas about what might be done to solve them. Therefore, one would expect that by now participation of the poor and marginalized would be an integral element of the work of all international donor agencies, recipient governments, NGOs and other private development organizations, which develop projects designed to benefit the poor.

In fact, the reality is quite the opposite. There have, however, been years of experimentation with the participation of the poor in projects and policy formulation processes. This work has been carried out by all the donor agencies discussed in this book and has yielded many insights. Nevertheless, important challenges remain. This chapter reviews these experiences at different phases of the project cycle, noting where success has been achieved and where work still remains to be done.

The Project Cycle

The focus of most donor attention regarding participation has been on the various phases of the project cycle – the period of time during which a project is first formulated, then designed, negotiated with the recipient government, implemented, monitored and evaluated. As noted in Chapter 1, these are artificial phases, created for bureaucratic convenience and often in conflict with the actual progression of a project's development. For purposes of description and analysis, we use the donor project cycle phases in this book. For simplicity, we use four major phases that are explained in Chapter 1. These are *identification* (also called *formulation*), *design* (also called *planning* or *preparation*), *implementation* and *evaluation*.

There are various participatory mechanisms used in project and policy work. For purposes of uniformity, the six delineated by the World Bank's Learning Group are used throughout this book. These are described in Chapter 1. Starting with least stakeholder involvement and ending with most, they are *information-sharing*, *consultation, joint assessment, shared decision-making, collaboration,* and *empowerment.*

It is instructive to examine the level of participation in each phase of the project cycle and consider the different points of view regarding such participation on the part of donors and the Working Group. But first it is important to note that the project identification phase often draws on information contained in earlier policy work or feasibility studies. Therefore the poor should be involved in the formulation of such policies or studies. Their participation in policy development is discussed later in this chapter.

Identification Phase
Although there is a growing acceptance by the World Bank, DFID and GTZ of the need and value of participation of the poor, there is very little such participation in this phase. It is in this phase that many fundamental decisions are made regarding the overall thrust of the project. Therefore, information dissemination to primary stakeholders regarding applicable policies and key facts is essential. Moreover, information provided *by* primary stakeholders in this phase is essential to developing a project that will be designed to address their needs and the economic and social conditions in their locality. It is also the time when a decision-making role by primary stakeholders would lead to the establishment of trust between them and staff from the government implementing agency and/or the donor organization. Moreover, such involvement would help them begin to develop a sense of 'ownership' of the project, important for their continued involvement throughout the subsequent phases and essential for sustainability of the endeavour after external funding has ceased. All of this is common sense, yet rarely are the poor involved.

Attitudes and development approaches explain why so much project formulation is faulty. For example, in a variety of interview settings, many World Bank staff have said that the reason they don't want to involve the poor before the project preparation phase is to avoid raising expectations. 'A tension, therefore, is created by including participation at the identification or pre-identification stage, and thus raising primary stakeholder expectation long before projects will begin activities' (Aycrigg, 1998).

Such fears reveal two problems. The first concerns the attitude and orientation of World Bank staff to the project. They consider it proper to have or share control with borrower government officials over the project framework and decisions in the formulation stage but assume (implicitly, at least) that there is no value in involvement of the poor at this point. Then, in the preparation phase, they make room for the primary stakeholders to have a say in how the project goes forward. 'Participation during preparation results in some tinkering around the edges of an already defined project, when it is too late for primary stakeholder views and concerns to be factored into project design' (Aycrigg, 1998).

The second problem is the need for reform of a project cycle that can take two years or more before any project activity begins. Appropriate project development would enable a slow phase-in of activities and a gradual infusion of funds to start such activities.

Specific data available from donor agencies are quite limited regarding levels of participation in each project phase. Based on donor comments and the data provided by the World Bank, DFID and GTZ, however, it is safe to say that participation of the poor in this phase seldom occurs. According to the DFID study: 'At present primary stakeholders have only marginal involvement in project identification, planning and design, since proposals are often prepared by programme managers and expatriate consultants' (INTRAC, 1998). GTZ reported that 'primary stakeholder groups or their representatives are rarely involved in the identification of a project' (Forster, 1998).

Data used by the World Bank's OED to evaluate levels of participation in projects from 1994–1998 show similar findings regarding the identification phase: a four-year average of 12 per cent participation by the poor (design phase – 31 per cent; implementation – 39 per cent and evaluation – 9 per cent).

These World Bank data are questionable for a number of reasons. The information was drawn from project appraisal documents which are written after the identification phase but before implementation, mainly to show what is *intended* in the project. Although these reports presumably have recorded actual participation in the identification phase, the data are not altogether reliable because of problems in how and what information was entered into the database. OED analysed the data because it represents the only database covering participation from 1994 to 1998 (Van Wicklin, 1998).

Rajesh Tandon points out that 'There is no question that involvement of primary stakeholders in project identification and early assessment is more complex than their involvement and engagement in the final planning and implementation of projects.' He goes on to say, however, that 'This is the lesson that needs to be addressed ... can we do something about the early steps of the project cycle ... but also on our methods and capacities to engage primary stakeholders at that stage' (Tandon, 1998a).

Not everyone agrees, however, on the importance of participation at this phase. For example: '... DFID tends to put more emphasis into that point [participation in the identification phase] but there is no evidence that there is a correlation between a lot of work at the design level and the final impact. There is a lot more correlation between good monitoring and a process approach to the project's having a positive impact' (Pratt, 1998).

Pratt later explained that although DFID and its partners had used participatory rural appraisal and other techniques at the identification, planning and design stages, the time gap before implementation started undermined this early participation. A DFID staff person had said to INTRAC at the time: 'If you start after a two-year gap, regardless of the work carried out before, you are starting with a blank sheet.' INTRAC's general conclusion was that far too much effort was being expended at this earlier phase, when what mattered was better monitoring during implementation to allow programme changes and adaptation. Although the theoretical ideal was to have participation as early as possible in the cycle, the reality of the project cycle defeated such an effort. Needs assessments were appropriate, in a general sense, but other activities at early phases had little impact on the overall progress of a programme (Pratt, pers comm).

What all seem to agree on is the need to undertake analysis at the beginning of the project identification phase in order to determine who the various stakeholders are, who will be affected positively or negatively by the project and who could influence the project either positively or negatively. Such an analysis could also reveal who might need capacity building assistance in order to participate in the development of the project. Such analysis is particularly important to determine gender roles and concerns so as to enable participation of women.

Few data are available from reports of most of the donor agencies regarding this particular issue. Where this was addressed regarding World Bank projects, the Working Group monitoring report revealed a need for improvement. As Rajesh Tandon noted at the 1998 conference, 'The first "challenge" for the project is a need for preparing more flexible and comprehensive project design, which includes at least an informal assessment of stakeholders, both primary and secondary, including the relationship that exists, and history of participation of primary stakeholders in the recent past. In some situations where this history was positive, efforts could be made to build on it. In situations where the history was negative, particularly the relationship between the community and the government implementing agency, some action needed to be taken before a positive environment for participation could be built' (Tandon, 1998a).

Regarding participation of women, in a recent assessment of participatory approaches in identification of World Bank projects, InterAction, the US consortium of NGOs, said:

> *Stakeholder analyses are instrumental in building capacity during project identification. If carried out with a gender perspective, in a participatory manner and in collaboration with governments and civil society, stakeholder analyses would strengthen the Bank's accountability to poor women and marginalized groups throughout the development of the project... . Gender analyses provide critical information on gender roles and institutional barriers to women's participation. The process of conducting these analyses enhances the capacity of affected groups to promote greater gender integration in both policy and project work.* (InterAction, 1999)

Donor agencies, NGOs and others have prepared a variety of excellent tools to assist those undertaking stakeholder analysis and other participatory processes (see Rietbergen-McCracken and Narayan, 1998).

Design Phase

Donor agencies report that participation of the poor in the preparation, design or planning phases of projects is quite good. For example, World Bank staff who contributed to the paper prepared for the November 1998 Participation Conference reported that stakeholder consultation in project preparation has become routine. 'People now understand that consultation and participation are key to project success' (Aycrigg, 1998). Given these comments, one would have expected a higher percentage in the World Bank's data on participation in the design phase, which was an average of 31 per cent from 1994 to 1998. GTZ reported that '... intended beneficiaries are consulted on project design in less than 10% of the projects (often in case of a preceding project)' (Forster, 1998a).

Although participation of the poor may be more frequent in this phase, the level of participation may not be particularly meaningful. According to GTZ, 'It is during the project planning phase when primary stakeholders are increasingly consulted and informed on the intended project. Involvement in decision-making, however, remains limited to a small part of projects, mainly those who start with an open orientation phase or extended planning advice to partner organizations' (Forster, 1998).

Implementation Phase

Generally speaking, those involved in development recognize the importance of participation by the poor in the implementation phase of development projects. Most donor agencies indicate substantial involvement in this phase, although data are very limited.

GTZ indicates that it is only at the start of the first implementation phase that the poor take part in decision-making. 'At this time, the majority of projects seriously engage in joint learning and facilitation processes at primary stakeholder level. Subsequently, the need may arise to accommodate beneficiaries' priorities' (Forster, 1998a). GTZ then gets caught in its own project cycle rigidities. 'If the joint learning process with primary stakeholders results in major re-orientations of the project plan, renegotiations between GTZ and BMZ become necessary. As this implies a major administrative effort, it is frequently delayed until the next implementation phase or even avoided at all' (Forster, 1998a).

A form of participation that has been more or less universally accepted is that expressed through cash contributions or in-kind services to the project by the poor. This usually takes place in the implementation phase. Cash or in-kind services are understood as ways to create a sense of ownership on the part of the poor, as well as obvious ways to cover some of the costs or carry out some of the work of the project. (Some time ago, this was the main way participation was understood by many in the donor community.) The assumption is that if primary stakeholders are not financially engaged in a project, they will not value the project's benefits or, in some cases, use or maintain them. If primary stakeholders are expected to provide cash or in-kind services for projects in which they have had no say, however, they may have just as limited a sense of ownership. What tends to be the case is that if primary stakeholders do have a serious role in the identification phase, they are more often than not quite willing to invest resources in the project.

Evaluation Phase

Just as there is little participation of the poor in the earliest phase of project formulation, likewise, there is almost no involvement in monitoring during the project, or during evaluation afterwards. In fact, according to reports presented, there is inadequate monitoring or evaluation of any kind going on in projects, let alone participatory monitoring and evaluation! To be clear about the phases, *monitoring* is carried out during the implementation of a project, whereas *evaluation* is conducted after the project has been completed.

GTZ had two revealing comments. First, in commenting on the level of participatory monitoring and evaluation, their report indicates '… the percentage of GTZ-supported projects actively involving primary stakeholders in monitoring and evaluation is quite low' (Forster, 1998a).

The second comment reveals a wider problem with evaluation. In his presentation at the Participation Conference, Reiner Forster said: '… We have to invest more in evaluating the impact of participation. Actually, we don't know what the impact of participatory approaches are at the moment' (Forster, 1998b).

The World Bank's statistics reveal similarly low percentages of intended participation of the poor in evaluation. Their four-year average from 1994 to 1998 was a paltry nine per cent (Van Wicklin, 1998).

A related problem is that in many cases international donor agencies do not focus enough attention on long-term impact. Impact evaluation is essential in development – that is, reviewing a project intervention five or ten years after all funding has ceased and outside assistance has been withdrawn. Otherwise, the development impact on the project's intended beneficiaries, their communities and sub-region cannot be determined. Furthermore, international workshops on evaluating social development in recent years have determined that it is just not possible to evaluate impact without qualitative data based on primary stakeholder responses and feedback. Quantitative results-based data alone are not enough (Pratt, 2000).

A final aspect concerning monitoring, evaluation, results and impact is the topic of accountability. International donor agencies consider themselves most accountable to their parliament or congress – and indirectly to taxpayers of the donor country, since it is taxpayer money that funds the donor agency's programme of assistance to recipient countries. As Brian Pratt said in his presentation of the evaluation of DFID: 'We did find that the project cycle management was not very supportive of participation. It is designed for Whitehall, for London, (for the executive branch of government, which is, in turn, accountable to Parliament), rather than for the clients' (Pratt, 1998). Of course, staff also feel accountable towards their supervisors in the donor agency, itself – according to traditional hierarchical accountability associated with project completion and job performance.

International donor agencies do not view themselves as accountable to the poor in the same way that they do to their governments and parliaments, although they want their projects to be successful in terms of benefits to them. This absence of accountability is a problem that donors are beginning to address. Andrew Norton from DFID said at the Participation Conference, 'We're also investigating ideas of social accountability because we recognize that looking at these issues institutionally is not simply about new approaches for management systems and procedures. It's about new approaches to our own accountability' (Norton, 1998).

Advances in accountability mechanisms, such as the establishment of an inspection panel at the World Bank and efforts now going on in the European Union to create a complaints procedure, have come about through insistent advocacy by NGOs. The Inspection Panel at the World Bank, which gives affected citizens redress over grievances related to World Bank-funded projects in their countries, was created only after several years of advocacy by NGOs and their skilful lobbying of Northern government parliaments to help in this effort (see Chapter 2).

Use of Participatory Mechanisms in Project Cycle Phases

This section looks at the different kinds of participation donors have used in phases of the project cycle and how effective they have been. Of the six mechanisms discussed, the first three promote *instrumental* participation, while the last three promote *transformational* participation (see Chapter 1 for definitions.) As the Working Group monitoring report states:

> *While transformation is the ultimate goal of participatory processes, and most civil society organizations focus their efforts on this, yet the elements of instrumental participation are important as well. In some ways, one prepares the base for the other. For example, the structures, methods, medium and language in which information is made available also affects its understanding by primary stakeholders. It was therefore considered important to focus attention on all the six mechanisms of promoting participation.* (Tandon and Cordeiro, 1998)

Information Disclosure and Dissemination

The most important first step in project formulation is informing the poor regarding the policy framework and key information about the project idea. The World Bank, DFID and USAID have made varying amounts of progress regarding information disclosure since NGOs first began lobbying for this at the World Bank in 1983. Although donors now frequently state that information must be shared with all stakeholders to engage them fully in development work, there is still much room for improvement. (How NGO advocacy succeeded in a World Bank decision to issue a new information disclosure policy in 1994 is described in Chapter 2.)

As the Working Group monitoring report on World Bank projects shows, unless an intermediary NGO, a donor agency staff person or government official in the country provides the available policy information to the primary stakeholders, they probably will not get it. At the present time, this is rarely done. Therefore, if primary stakeholders are invited to become involved in formulation of a project, they will operate at a disadvantage on two counts:

1   They may not have had any involvement in the formulation of the development policy for the particular sector, or any other policies of either the government or the donor agency involved which have a bearing on the intended project. Nor may they have seen any of the documentation concerning such policies.
2   They probably will not have information other than what donor agency or recipient government personnel tell them about the intended project.

As Rajesh Tandon reported regarding the Working Group monitoring of World Bank projects at the November 1998 Participation Conference: 'We were not clear with the level of information dissemination directly carried out with primary stakeholders. ... In some cases we noticed that information disclosure to secondary stakeholders was carried out but that did not trickle down ... or spread, or engage primary stakeholders in information dissemination' (Tandon, 1998a). Of the nine projects discussed in the Working Group monitoring report, information sharing *directly* with primary stakeholders occurred in only two of them (the District Primary Education Project in India [DPEP II] and the Community-based Natural Resource and Wildlife Management Project [GEPRENAF] in Côte d'Ivoire). In these two, such information sharing was done only in the appraisal phase (Tandon and Cordeiro, 1998).

Later in the conference, Gloria Davis, former Director of the Social Development Department of the World Bank, said in her presentation of the World Bank's record on participation:

> *What's the key element in all of this? For me, it's information. If I were you, what I'd be telling Mr Wolfensohn is that we need to be very systematic about how we disseminate information. That it's the basis, the starting point. In every country we need to be sure that citizens have access*

to information about projects which may affect them and about development programmes that are going to have an impact upon them. This is absolutely essential. This is something you can help us do. (Davis, 1998)

Consultative Mechanisms

Consultation is normally carried out through meetings, field visits or interviews. Of the projects included in the Working Group report, two-thirds of them indicated that primary stakeholders were consulted at different stages of the project.

The Rural Initiatives and Poverty Relief (PROINDER) Project in Argentina, which was monitored by the Working Group, includes a good example of consultation in the appraisal and diagnosis phase.

Participatory diagnosis workshops were held, comple-mented by a study of existing statistics on rural poverty and of relevant case studies. The workshops involved, in turn, representatives of provincial governments, NGOs, and primary stakeholders. Some workshops specifically involved rural women and members of women's groups to have a gender perspective on rural poverty. Others targeted indigenous or migrant workers. Overall, very useful information was rapidly collected.

Unfortunately, the monitoring report continues:

The only proposals from beneficiaries which were accepted by the program were those meeting the condi-tions set beforehand by the Bank, and ... neither the government nor the beneficiaries were familiar with such limitations.

Department of Agriculture officials noted the danger of raising stake-holders' expectations and not being able to fulfill them (Housing and Social Service Organization (SEHAS), 1998).

Joint Assessment

Participatory assessments, evaluations and beneficiary assessments are ways in which joint assessment is carried out in projects. Of the projects reported on by the Working Group, in only three projects were primary stakeholders involved in such work. Such assessments can be used at various points along the project cycle.

Examples of primary stakeholder participation in joint assessment were noted in the District Primary Education Program (DPEP II) in Madhya Pradesh, India, which was monitored by the Working Group. In the planning stage of the project, communities were involved in planning how the programme would be implemented through participatory exercises. All districts were covered through this effort, but the 1997 monitoring report showed that only the most influential people, such as the *sarpanches*, who are the heads of the *Panchayat* (the local self-governance institutions) and teachers, participated actively. Women were hardly involved. However:

> the Total Literacy Campaign, which had been initiated by the government as part of its earlier National Literacy Mission, was essential in leading to community participation: it helped selecting volunteers and popularizing the need for literacy and the community was deeply involved. (Samarthan-Centre for Development Support, 1998)

Shared Decision Making

In five of the nine projects reported on by the Working Group, primary stakeholders were involved in joint planning and decision making. Such joint efforts only began in the design phase and extended through the implementation phase, however. In only one project was joint decision making by primary stakeholders included in the monitoring phase.

The Second Rural Communal Irrigation Development Project (CIDP-II) in the Philippines reveals a good example of shared decision-making. In the design phase, irrigation associations (communal groups of farmers and water users) participated in the process of designing the project, and their inputs were incorporated into the final plan. It should be noted that this project is a follow-on effort to the CIDP-I, which ran from 1982 to 1989 and was the first foreign-assisted irrigation project in the Philippines focusing wholly on the development of communal systems and farmer participation (Korten and Siy, 1998). Thus, CIDP-II has had to strive to live up to the high standards of participation set during this past project (Philippines Rural Reconstruction Movement, 1998).

Collaboration

Joint committees, working groups or task forces are ways in which collaboration takes place. In some instances, certain stakeholders can be given principal responsibility for implementation. Although all projects reported on by the Working Group indicated collaboration by primary stakeholders, this was almost entirely in the implementation phase. In only two of the projects did primary stakeholders collaborate in the planning or monitoring stages.

The aim of the GEPRENAF Project in Côte d'Ivoire was to enable primary stakeholders to diversify their livelihoods, improve their living standards and help preserve wildlife and bio-diversity. Their associations were to be progressively constituted, beginning with village associations and then formalizing into inter-village associations. During implementation, these associations did play an important role. The monitoring report notes:

> *In the Warigue project area, village groups had been identified and encouraged to form village associations. In one district, inter-village associations have been constituted. In the Mont Tingui area, four committees for the attribution of funds ... have been created. Three ... deal with local development issues and include representatives from all the villages of the project area. The other one deals with bio-diversity conservation and includes a land-owning representative from each village as well as representatives of the migrant population. Awareness building has been addressed through the information, education, and communication program aimed at sensibilising the population to issues such as wildlife management, bush fire control or village organization for project management. This has favored the opening up of paths around the bio-diversity area by villagers on contract. Informal surveillance by villagers through their own initiative has also developed.* (INADES-Formation, 1998)

Empowerment and Capacity Building

In the Working Group monitoring reports, only two of the projects had given any attention to empowerment and capacity building of primary stakeholders. It should be noted that none of the projects monitored had reached the evaluation stage.

An example of effective capacity building from the Working Group reports comes from the CIDP-II in the Philippines. This project had effective primary stakeholder participation in all phases except for the identification phase. The capacity building provided consisted of workshops built into the project design. The workshops were held to enable the irrigation associations to formulate their own water distribution plans, maintenance plans and conflict management plans. Representatives of the Provincial Irrigation Offices facilitated the workshops. The monitoring report did note a tendency to 'short circuit the capacity building processes, presumably to reduce costs' (Philippines Rural Reconstruction Movement, 1998).

Because participatory processes are not a systematic part of project formulation or design in most donor agencies or recipient governments, capacity building is necessary for all participants, not just the poor. Donor agency and recipient government staff, and NGOs in some instances, need to learn how to facilitate participatory processes in formulation and design of projects. Formulating participatory projects requires the ability to adapt plans and expectations as new information becomes available, rather than imposing a plan based on expert knowledge about the particular sector.

For the poor, the focus of capacity building ought to include not only project-related issues such as proper management or financial record keeping. The orientation towards capacity building should be more on the long term, as a way to empower primary stakeholders to mobilize community involvement, build and run local institutions effectively and become more effective participants in development. Again, Tandon addressed this issue as regards World Bank projects: 'Systematic and up-front commitment to do capacity building with primary and secondary stakeholders, to engage them in an informed and systematic manner in participation processes for a given project was missing and needs to be emphasized' (Tandon, 1998a, p13).

The Working Group's written report on the projects monitored noted that the capacity building that did take place for primary stakeholders was focused primarily on project-specific issues. The report recommended that:

> *The focus of capacity building must be on strengthening primary stakeholders' abilities to* 'nfluence and share control over development decisions and resources which affect them' *as the Bank says, and not just on being better users of facilities or benefits which projects offer to them.* (Tandon and Cordeiro, 1998)

The 1998 Participation Conference workshop held on capacity building was quite specific regarding the kinds of skills which should be encouraged. Capacity building efforts should:

1   Enhance the human and material base of social organizations, in order to lay the foundation for sustainable capacity, and not just

the superstructures, that is, the organizations themselves. This requires tackling issues such as poverty, political exclusion and social discrimination so that people have the basic security and voice to represent themselves in project and policy processes.

2 Recognize and build on existing or indigenous capacities and perceptions of what capacities are required. The starting point should always be to ask people the simple questions, 'What sort of capacities do you want? What's already there? What do you feel should be the priority?' Start with this rather than automatically importing packages or capacities thought from the outside to be important.

3 Keep in the community a variety of important capacities, such as collecting and analysing data for use in planning, and developing self-assessment models, for example. Such skills are basic building blocks for other capacities that are often ignored. More often, donors extract data from the community without leaving behind the skills or the data for the community to use for itself.

4 Encourage stronger organizational capacities such as the ability to link and work with other social movements, banks, governments and donors for example.

5 Give priority to efforts to enhance the capacities of women's organizations and gender awareness in all organizations working at the community level.

6 Give communities access to timely and accurate information about the influence communities are likely to have, for example, on formulation of a particular project. They should be assisted in identifying how to influence donor policies and procedures, and their expectations should be dealt with in a straightforward, responsible manner.

7 Distinguish between capacities related to representation as opposed to capacities for contracting with government or donor agencies.

Interestingly, when the workshop group attempted to note best practices, they were unable to cite many concrete examples. This is, perhaps, symptomatic of the dearth of appropriate capacity building being done (Group Three, 1998).

This review of levels and kinds of participation used in the projects monitored by the Working Group shows consistency with data collected elsewhere by the World Bank. Participation by the poor in the formulation and monitoring phases was quite limited, while involvement in the planning phase was somewhat better, and quite substantial in the implementation phase.

Another finding from the reports is consistent with World Bank data collected elsewhere. Even in instances where the poor were involved in four project cycle phases, and participated through four of the six basic mechanisms, the quality of the participation was often unsatisfactory. The report of the GEPRENAF Project in Côte d'Ivoire, in which the poor participated extensively, says: 'Apart from during the implementation stage, primary stakeholders' participation consisted mainly ... in providing the project officials with information. Neither have they access to strategic documents nor have they any decision-making power' (INADES-Formation, 1998). The report does show some effort to respond to this complaint by noting that: 'Project officials reacted to this statement by proposing to make simplified versions of the strategic documents available to the population as part of the village dossier' (INADES-Formation, 1998).

Participants at the 1998 Participation Conference generally agreed that more work needs to be done by all the donors regarding these two important topics: to increase involvement of the poor in all phases of projects, especially formulation and monitoring, and to improve the quality of participation.

The Role of Secondary Stakeholders

The World Bank, GTZ, DFID, Sida and USAID all work directly with and through recipient government institutions and place emphasis on personnel of these agencies as the most important secondary stakeholders, either in central ministries or at the local government level.

In reviewing participation efforts of the various donor agencies, it seems clear that not enough attention has been paid to helping government implementing agencies and their personnel become convinced of the value of participatory approaches, and to acquire the skills to carry out such processes. On the positive side, Sida has done pioneering work in this area (see Chapter 5). More typical, however, is the case of the World Bank, which defines its clients as recipient governments and professes a commitment to participation. When asked about responsibilities for instituting participatory processes, many World Bank staff say it is definitely the recipient government's responsibility. However, there seems to be much too little attention paid to either helping convince government personnel of the importance of participation, or providing training or other assistance needed to do participatory work. Even with such assistance, participation probably will not become rooted in the agency unless there are significant reforms in operations and the attitudes of government personnel.

Brian Pratt noted this problem in his presentation at the Participation Conference. In discussing INTRAC's review of DFID, he said:

> *The first thing to emerge was that the recent focus on primary stakeholders has led to the neglect of secondary stakeholders. Their participation is crucial to the development of projects. Official agencies ignore them at their peril.*

He went on to say that:

> *If an official agency wishes to see improved primary stakeholder participation, this will most likely come through improved relationships with the local secondary stakeholders who still have responsibility for implementing programmes and assuring their sustainability... It is possible to have an excellent project, but if these are not fully supported by the host institutions and mainstreamed into the whole ministry or department, they become, as one of our respondents put it, 'islands of excellence in a sea of chaos.* (Pratt, 1998)

Changes Needed in the Project Cycle

What is revealed when analysing donor practices is that project cycles and procedures do not allow for the time and flexibility needed to carry out a participatory project. This is particularly so in the early phases of a project, when trust must be established between the poor and donor or government representatives; lengthy processes of information gathering and consultation must take place, and changes need to be made based on new information or changing circumstances.

Over the years, many donors have developed standard procedures to use in project development. These tend to be more suited to the bureaucratic needs of the donor agency than to the stakeholders who stand to benefit – or lose – from the projects. DFID and GTZ both use the 'Logical Framework' (LOGFRAME), originally developed, but since abandoned, by USAID. The LOGFRAME is a tool in developing a project that outlines what is to be done and the expected outcomes of project activities. Once developed, project personnel continue to use this model as a guide during the project. It often becomes a kind of straightjacket and works against project effectiveness because it limits flexibility and the ability to change course if needed. As Brian Pratt said: 'Although participation can be carried out in projects using the LOGFRAME, participatory elements tend to be the first victims of the procedural imperatives of such results-based systems' (Pratt, pers comm, 2000). The World Bank, through its project cycle, uses a 'blueprint' approach to project development, which carries with it rigidities similar to those of the LOGFRAME. For its part, Sida has used a more flexible project framework for several years (Rudqvist, 1992).

Procurement mechanisms used by the donors vary somewhat by agency. NGOs, which often serve as intermediaries between the poor and donor agencies, are accorded some flexibility through grants made by bilateral agencies. In some instances, however, such as USAID, there is a growing preference for 'cooperative agreements', which provide for more involvement in implementation decisions by USAID staff and carry with them more onerous oversight mechanisms. The World Bank's procurement system traditionally has allowed almost no flexibility, with NGOs in client countries expected to go through a standard tendering process for contracts let by the recipient government. The World Bank has relaxed its procurement procedures as a result of the 1994 participation report, although there are still problems.

Some of the donors have begun to make changes in the project cycle to accommodate these needs, but much more is needed. USAID has made significant changes in its programme to provide more flexibility in project development and implementation. But what they have discovered is that even with new procedures in place, some staff create new rigidities through the way they use the new procedures. This indicates that, along with such changes, there must be training and guidelines given to staff to encourage them to use the new procedures.

The World Bank has begun using learning and innovation loans and adaptable programme lending on a pilot basis to adjust the project cycle to needs of client governments. The loans can be approved by World Bank management, rather than the Board, cannot exceed US$5 million, and are intended to provide support to promising pilot initiatives or to experiment with local models prior to launching larger-scale interventions or to carry out capacity building. These loans are conducive to participation and are a promising start, but they have not been evaluated, and, as yet, represent a very small percentage of World Bank loan money. The bulk of World Bank projects are still being designed according to the old project cycle. Moreover, according to World Bank staff comments, whether participation is included depends very much on the orientation of the manager in charge of the particular project.

In 1992, GTZ instituted what they call an *open orientation phase* in their project planning cycle for complex projects to enable the requesting government organization to take the time necessary to involve important stakeholders and agree with them on a project design and implementation plan. These open orientations can take as long as two to three years; and the planning processes are supported by GTZ advisers in the particular country. For less complex projects, new procedures were also instituted in 1992 to allow for up to six months to do participatory project preparations, as opposed to the earlier three to four weeks (Forster, 1998a).

Such changes are encouraging. Vastly more effort must be made by donor agencies, however, to reform their procedures and procurement arrangements so as to align them with the rhythms and processes of participatory projects. Research has shown that in cases where the poor have been successfully involved in large-scale initiatives, donor procedures and funding practices were adapted to accommodate the evolutionary nature of such projects (Thompson, 1995).

Perhaps the most important lesson learned in this ten-year period by staff of international donor organizations is that involvement of the poor in the formulation of development policies is essential for successful projects. The choice of location, thematic emphasis and other important aspects of projects are shaped significantly by prior policy work. Thus, the poor need to be involved in these policy processes to provide local knowledge and alternative perspectives.

Consultation with the poor in formulation of development policies – virtually unheard of ten years ago – has begun and is increasingly being undertaken by international donor agencies. There are a growing number of examples in the World Bank's country assistance strategies (CAS), GTZ's policy work, USAID's country strategic plans, and DFID's new focus on involvement of the poor in sector policy formulation. We now turn to a review of these experiences of participation in policy formulation. The focus is primarily on World Bank policy formulation since the World Bank has been the major target of NGO advocacy in this regard.

PARTICIPATION IN FORMULATION OF DEVELOPMENT POLICIES

Ten years ago, it rarely crossed anyone's mind in an international donor agency to consult with the poor or representatives of civil society organizations (CSO) in formulation of development policy. This process was, and to a large extent, still is done by development 'experts' in consultation with recipient government representatives. Therefore, what is surprising is the amount of progress that has been made in just a few years in engaging NGOs and CSOs – and in a few cases, the poor, themselves – in consultations regarding development policy formulation.

When international donor agencies began to recognize the value and need for participation of the poor in development, they started efforts to incorporate participation in projects. For some donor agencies, such as GTZ, this was completely logical since a project focus was, and is, their main purpose. For other donors, however, policies have as much, if not more, influence than projects in shaping development approaches.

Donor agencies began to accept the need to engage CSOs and the poor in formulation of development policies about four years ago as a result of more than 15 years of advocacy by NGOs. The origin of these efforts was in the early 1980s when the World Bank began applying structural adjustment programmes to recipient countries. NGOs decided early on that these were undemocratic: at worst they were inappropriate ways to improve economic performance and at best were necessary medicine whose side-effects were devastating to the poor.

Year after year, NGOs tenaciously advocated that the World Bank should halt these programmes, and devise an alternative formula that would be more appropriate. They argued that citizens of the countries concerned should be involved in designing such an alternative together with the governments.

After several years of NGO advocacy, the World Bank acknowledged the negative effects of the structural adjustment programmes on the poor by creating 'compensatory' programmes. These were short-term projects that created temporary jobs for people being laid off from parastatal companies that were being 'privatized'. These early programmes evolved into social investment funds that engage the poor in small-scale infrastructure and job creation efforts, although mostly in the implementation of these projects rather than in their formulation or design.

After more than 15 years of NGO advocacy regarding structural adjustment, the value of involving the poor and CSOs in the formulation of development policies began to gather momentum. NGOs at that time focused on two major targets:

1   The first was an effort by NGOs around the world to convince the World Bank to undertake a process of tripartite engagement to review the effects of structural adjustment in various countries.

SAPRI (see Chapter 2), which was launched in July 1997, involves the World Bank, the recipient government and the citizens of the country through their NGOs and civil society organizations in reviewing results of structural adjustment programmes already implemented and in making recommendations for future economic policies.

2 The second target was the development of the World Bank's CAS for work to be carried out in a particular country which is developed in consultation with the recipient government.

In 1995, NGOs began to advocate that NGOs and other civil society organizations should be involved in the formulation of the CAS in recipient countries, and that the draft strategy be made public.

These efforts on the part of NGOs have begun to bear fruit. In 1995, virtually no NGOs, civil society representatives or the poor were consulted by the World Bank or their governments in the formulation of the CAS. According to a recent Bank review, 40 per cent of strategies developed in 1999 and 2000 had a high level of participation (Shah and Tikare, 1999) Nevertheless, serious concerns remain regarding the process and quality of such consultations as well as their results.

Policy Processes

In addition to the CAS, the World Bank and other large donor agencies have begun to incorporate participation of civil society and the poor into other policy processes. At the World Bank, these include certain of the policies included in economic and sector work. Although the World Bank has expanded its consultation with various stakeholder groups in sector policy formulation, most of the attention it has focused on the poor has been through participatory poverty assessments: 43 such assessments have been conducted since 1993 (Aycrigg, 1998). The World Bank made a new participatory effort in 1999. This was a special study called 'Consultations with the Poor', designed as an input to the *World Development Report 2000* (WDR–2000) on poverty. The goal was to enable a wide range of poor people in diverse countries and conditions to contribute to the concepts and content of the WDR–2000. The study focused on poor peoples' perceptions in four areas: well-being and ill-being as defined and experienced by poor people; problems and priorities of different groups; the role of public, civic and market institutions in people's lives; and gender relations. A part of this research was a participatory field study to collect information from the poor in 23 countries (Narayan et al, 2000).

Participation in Policy Formulation

Some of the large donor agencies have begun to incorporate participation of the poor into policy formulation and the most extensive monitoring of this has been carried out by the Working Group regarding the World Bank's country assistance strategy. Thus, the following analysis focuses on results of this work.

Information Disclosure and Dissemination

Perhaps the most fundamental way for participation by NGOs, CSOs and the poor to occur is for them to have the same information as those who are consulting with them regarding a particular development policy. World Bank information is now available on policies concerning environmental assessments, analyses and action plans; final results of economic and sector work; sectoral policy papers; and legal opinions of the General Council. In fact, this information is available on the Internet (Aycrigg, 1998).

In August 1998, the World Bank's Board agreed that after Board discussion of the country assistance strategy, and with consent of the government, the World Bank should release a public information notice describing its main elements. Furthermore, when governments request, the World Bank may fully disclose the strategy (Aycrigg, 1998).

At present, draft strategy papers are shared with NGOs and civil society organizations who are consulted during the period in which the strategy is being developed. There is a great deal of room for improvement, however, as there are no systems in place to ensure timely access to such documents.

If consultations with NGOs and CSOs or the poor are to be useful and productive, they need to receive information with sufficient lead time to read it and hold preparatory meetings with constituencies or other groups. If individuals are invited as representatives of their organizations or networks (farmers, women's groups, trade unions etc), they need to be able to share the information with their constituencies and hold discussions in order to get their input prior to the consultations. In fact, it can be counterproductive to provide written information at the time of the consultations or a day or two before. Such a practice leads to the suspicion that the consultation is simply a public relations effort.

In many instances, no feedback was provided to the participants about results of the consultations, nor about what was ultimately included in the strategy. This was the case with the poor in Kenya and Uganda, and NGOs in India, Peru and Ghana. As a result, most organizations involved felt a sense of frustration and lack of continuity in the consultation process (Tandon and Cordeiro, 1998).

Consultations

Although there are still many aspects to improve in consultations with CSOs and the poor, some progress is being made. A World Bank review of CASs developed in 1997 and 1998 showed some degree of participation in 26 of 47 strategies approved by the Board. An in-depth review of 22 of these revealed that ten of them:

- included extensive consultation with a broad array of civil society representatives;
- involved civil society in the planning of the exercise;
- reached out to rural areas; and
- planned feedback or follow-up.

This represented 45 per cent of the 22 participatory strategies and 21 per cent of all 47 strategies in the sample. This was a significant increase of participation in consultation for strategy formulation since a smaller survey had been undertaken two years before (Clark and Dorschel, 1998). As more participation is built in to such processes, improvements are being made and World Bank staff are learning from their mistakes. The following examples show the progression:

- In several cases, the duration of the consultation was inadequate for the scope and importance of the issues to be considered. Among strategies monitored by the Working Group, the duration of the meetings in the case of Ghana, Uganda, Nepal, Bangladesh and India ranged from one hour to one day (Tandon and Cordeiro, 1998).
- In Kenya and Vietnam, however, there were sustained discussions over a few months, as a result of which the NGOs consulted felt that their concerns had been considered (Tandon and Cordeiro, 1998).

The quality and process of consultations have varied significantly from one country to another, based primarily on individual World Bank staff and their level of interest and knowledge of interactive processes. What is also apparent from these cases is that consultation regarding CASs may be more effective or at least more manageable:

> *in smaller countries such as Vietnam, or in heavily indebted countries, such as Kenya. In larger countries, such as India, participatory and transparent CAS processes face greater resistance, as well as greater*

challenges given the size and complexity of the country.
(Tandon and Cordeiro, 1998)

Changes in the CASs Resulting from Consultations

According to the World Bank, in no less than ten cases in which civil society organizations or the poor were consulted, the assistance strategy was altered in significant respects as a result of such discussions. In a few cases, the overall orientation of the strategy was changed. In others, issues were added that had not been in the draft prior to the consultation, or the orientation or direction of a particular issue was changed due to what was learned in the consultation. For example:

- The Kenya strategy changed from viewing participation as an instrumental process confined to its preparation to seeing participation as a long-term strategy to achieve the objectives of public-sector reform (Aycrigg, 1998).
- The Bangladesh strategy focused on institutional aspects of economic growth and poverty reduction, and specifically on the role of civil society and the private sector in the delivery of basic services and infrastructure development (Aycrigg, 1998).
- As a result of consultation, the primary focus of the Colombia strategy was changed to address issues of violence and public insecurity (Aycrigg, 1998).

Changes Needed in Policy Formulation

The way many consultations have been carried out thus far, as stated earlier, has led to frustration on the part of NGOs, civil society representatives and the poor. The following suggestions from the Working Group are offered as ways to improve the process.

1 *Diversity of stakeholders.* The country assistance stratey consultation process needs to be more inclusive of diverse perspectives in a country. Rather than just consulting with NGOs or the poor, the World Bank should broaden the process to include a larger perspective of civil society, such as trade unions, women's groups, research institutions, academics and people's movements.
2 *Criteria for selection.* It is important to make known the criteria against which individuals are chosen to be participants in the consultation, including whether the criteria vary depending on the kinds of stakeholders invited. This will reassure people that there is a logic to the choice being made, and that those chosen are not simply people already known to the World Bank or who live in

the capital city or are more likely to agree with the orientation of the World Bank or the borrower government.

3 *Inclusion of Analysis of Earlier Strategies.* Evaluating past strategies should inform the preparation process of current ones.
4 *Inclusion of policy research and analysis related to social issues.* This should be considered as information to be used in the strategy in the same way as economic research is intended to be.
5 *Publication of the Country Assistance Strategy.* The strategy itself should be a public document that can be shared widely. This is not entirely within the jurisdiction of the World Bank, however, since national governments have a right to decide on this.
6 *Common Procedures.* The World Bank must ensure common procedures regarding participation of the poor in the preparation of strategies in all countries. Although directives and guidelines have been developed by the World Bank, procedures to ensure that this happens need to be enforced (Tandon and Cordeiro, 1998).

It is worth noting that reports collected by SAPRI in mid-2000 from NGOs in four countries in three regions where strategies were being formulated make most of these same recommendations.

PARTICIPATORY MECHANISMS AND PROCESSES

This review of participation in projects and policies has shown the progress made and the work still left to be done. There are significant efforts underway in a variety of organizations to improve participation of the poor in both projects and policy formulation. In the past 10 to 15 years, a number of mechanisms have been created to involve the poor in their own development. Participatory rural appraisal is probably the best known of these tools. Robert Chambers, one of its originators, describes it:

> *as a family of approaches, methods and behaviours that enable people to express and analyse the realities of their lives and conditions, to plan themselves what action to take, and to monitor and evaluate the results... The key elements of [Participatory Rural Appraisal] are the methods used, and – most importantly – the behaviour and attitudes of those who facilitate it.* (Chambers, 1996)

Participatory appraisal is now widely viewed as a way of engaging the poor in both project and policy formulation that will lead to better approaches to development in their communities. It can and has been abused or used inappropriately, however. As Chambers points out, in the appraisals it is the local people, themselves, who decide what to do with the information and analysis they generate. Sometimes outsiders have used the process unethically to extract information to use for their own purposes. 'Such practice is unethical because local people are brought into a process in which expectations are raised, and then frustrated, if no action or follow-up results' (Chambers, 1996).

GTZ uses participatory appraisals in a large number of projects.As noted in their report for the November 1998 Participation Conference, however: '... The majority of projects face difficulties in flexibly applying PRA. Project staff often perform a sequence of techniques in a standardised way without adaptation to the underlying purpose or questions' (Forster, 1998b). Introductory training courses apparently have not allowed staff to master the methods sufficiently to apply them flexibly and appropriately.

The GTZ experience underscores the need for long-term training for donor and government staff responsible for participatory processes. More important than learning how to use a 'mechanism' is the behavioural approach a person brings to participatory work: a willingness to listen, to keep an open mind, to be flexible, so that the poor reach their own conclusions about what is needed and about possible solutions.

A variety of other mechanisms exist to assist the poor in project or policy formulation. Some of these were noted in Chapter 1 or mentioned earlier in this chapter. They include stakeholder analysis, beneficiary assessments, SARAR and participatory monitoring and evaluation.

Although there are now many useful tools available, there is still much to be learned about how to involve the poor in project and policy formulation. CIDA addressed this question in its study prepared for the IGP (see Chapter 2). The study points out how much remains to be learned about the practice of participation, and notes at least eight areas where studies are needed and the agency which proposed the topic (CIDA, 1997):

1 how participatory methods are institutionalized in the whole of the project cycle and which planning, administrative, institutional or political problems emerge in the process of switching to a more participatory approach (GTZ);
2 a cross-sectoral study of the costs and benefits of participation throughout the life cycle of an aid-assisted activity (DFID);
3 which outcomes are produced by which kinds of participation (DFID);

4   how to grade and sequence project outputs in terms of the kind and amount of participation required (DFID);
5   the costs and benefits of participatory approaches to the organization as well as to other stakeholders (DFID);
6   how to accommodate results-based management and sustainable development policies (CIDA);
7   how to involve larger populations in participatory methods (IDS); and
8   how to design a matrix that links the phases of the project cycle, participatory methods and different types of projects (Inter-American Development Bank).

Unfortunately, the IGP did not function effectively for longer than about a year, and the CIDA study was never properly discussed by the IGP members. There continues to be the need for all donor agencies to incorporate participation into their operations, so that the 'how to' of participatory practice can be shared, understood and applied.

CONCLUSIONS AND GUIDELINES FOR THE FUTURE

This examination of the record of three donor agencies' efforts to involve the poor in projects and policy processes reveals several common themes. Although little primary stakeholder participation takes place in early and late phases of projects, a considerable amount now does occur in design and implementation. Second, although such participation is not the norm throughout the project cycles of these donor agencies, there has been extensive experimentation. At the World Bank, for example, although systematic incorporation of participation has not occurred (changes in procedures, rewards, the project cycle etc), its entrepreneurial environment has enabled interested staff to undertake participatory processes with primary stakeholders. This has also been the case in other agencies such as GTZ. What has been learned can now be used in these agencies to improve the quality of participation – if the political will exists.

It is also clear that donors must continue to adapt their project cycles to enable the poor to participate. GTZ's effort at 'open orientation phases' is a good beginning. The World Bank's learning and innovation loans and adaptable programme lending initiatives designed to provide borrower governments flexibility in early project identification, are conducive to participation in the hands of the right task manager. They are a step in the right direction and more should be done to improve them.

As for participation of civil society and the poor in the formulation of development policies, progress has occurred. The positive effects of such participation have been readily apparent to donor agency staff involved in these policy formulation exercises. Looking at the changes in the World Bank's CASs as a result of participation shows the impact such efforts can have. These processes begin to engage the poor with donors and national governments so that they could have a role in subsequent projects.

What is clear from this review is that a few basic guidelines need to be followed by all large donor agencies in project development and policy formulation. If followed, these would help significantly to give a sense of ownership to the poor and would enable the recipient government to get the greatest benefit from the investment of time and resources. The four guidelines are:

1 *All relevant information related to the project or policy should be shared in a timely fashion with all parties in the appropriate language.*
2 *Project development or policy formulation need to be carried out in an 'iterative' way by trial and error, feedback and with flexibility.* In projects, this enables stakeholders to agree on an approach, try it out, reflect on it and then make corrections based on feedback and new information. When formulating policy, such a process enables participants to see whether their ideas are being incorporated into subsequent drafts and can help foster a dynamic exchange on important national development issues. A by-product of such processes of working together is the development of relationships between all parties.
3 *Improve the skills of all stakeholders to engage in participatory project and policy development.* All stakeholders need to learn how to engage effectively with one another in processes of project development or policy formulation. Most especially, donors and secondary stakeholders need to adopt a learning approach and facilitative attitude towards their work with the poor. Related to this is the need for donors to play a more vigorous role in helping to change attitudes of recipient government personnel towards involvement of the poor and to assist in building their skills in participatory processes.
4 *Increase the quantity and improve the quality of participation by the poor.* Two of the most important lessons on which participants agreed at the 1998 Participation Conference are that much more has to be done to involve the poor in all phases of project development and in policy formulation, and that the quality of

such participation must be improved. All felt that a set of minimum quality standards should be developed. A willingness by donors to develop such standards would be an important step in committing themselves to fully incorporating participation. Such a process could trigger the structural and policy changes necessary to make the participation of the poor the norm in development projects and policy formulation.

Chapter 4

Incorporating Participation of the Poor in International Development Agencies

INTRODUCTION

Since its origins in the United States in the 1940s, the field of organizational development has become more widely understood around the world. For many years, the basic adaptations for successful organizational change have been applied extensively in private business and to a lesser extent in public institutions. This chapter examines organizational change and reflects on how well the World Bank and USAID have succeeded in adopting reforms and innovations to incorporate the participation of the poor into their work.

THE BASICS OF ORGANIZATIONAL CHANGE

First of all, why do organizations change? Motivating factors often come from both inside and outside the institution. Moreover, one set frequently influences the other.

Why Organizations Change

External Reasons

For donor organizations, factors promoting change can include shifts in the overall external environment as well as changes closer to the organization. Changes in the wider external environment can include new trends that signal to the organization that it should consider updating its work approaches or management styles. For example in the case of the World Bank, in the mid-1980s, important changes occurred in several countries as a result of people's own actions. All of these changes were occurring independently of efforts by donor agencies in these countries. Also noted earlier was the increase in NGOs calling attention to the need to involve poor communities in efforts to reduce poverty.

Other motivations for change external to the organization can be found closer to the organization. Decreases in external funding sources, dissatisfaction voiced by the organization's clients or 'customers', or criticism by outside organizations could be other reasons for change. In the case of the World Bank, NGOs had begun agitating for Bank reform in the early 1980s. Over several years, they increasingly urged it to focus on poverty reduction as its central mission and to alter design and implementation of large infrastructure projects such as dams in order to protect and preserve the environment and the rights of local people. NGOs had become public critics of the way the Bank conducted its business.

As for USAID, the US Government's decision to streamline government – carried out through the Government Performance Results Act (often referred to as the 'Results Act') – served as an opportunity for the agency to begin a reform effort, one it wished to carry out for its own internal reasons.

Internal Reasons

Motivations for change inside an organization can include dissatisfaction with the level or quality of results being achieved, inappropriate or outdated management practices, or outmoded technical approaches to the work of the organization. Symptoms of such problems can be low staff morale, low productivity, an increase in staff turnover, complaints by board members regarding organizational results or decreases in funding levels.

There were numerous internal reasons for change at USAID. For several years prior to the reform effort undertaken in 1993, the agency had suffered from a distinct lack of leadership. Many internal problems had been left unaddressed for several years and worsened as a result. These included poor financial systems resulting in poor accountability; cumbersome programme procedures and onerous procurement requirements. Monitoring and evaluation systems determined if projects were completed successfully, but could not measure impact on the projects' beneficiaries.

At the time that participation was first introduced at the World Bank, there were few internal motivations for change. A small number of it staff wanted more attention to participation as a way of increasing project effectiveness. Staff eager to take up the issue of participation, however, were responding primarily to external signals coming from democratization efforts in several countries mentioned earlier, their desire to focus the Bank more on poverty reduction, and to address NGO concerns for its reform.

How Organizations Change

Once an organization has identified the need to change, how does it go about it? Numerous books have now been written about how organizations change, grow and innovate. Some have become best sellers and the phrases coined in their pages have become common knowledge in organizations around the world. *In Search of Excellence* popularized slogans such as 'management by wandering around' (Peters and Waterman, 1982). This phrase captured the common-sense importance of a manager being constantly informed and in touch with everyday issues. A more recent book that many organizational development specialists have come to rely on is *The Fifth Discipline* (Senge, 1990), which discusses how to become a 'learning organization'. In this book, Senge discusses the need for organizations to change and continue to adapt to a constantly shifting environment. He outlines how organizations can do this by becoming learning organizations. The book talks of how instituting certain management practices, organizational procedures and operational behaviour will enable organizations to continuously grow and adapt to changing circumstances.

In very small organizations, changes may occur relatively easily. A new leader with a strong, exciting vision might succeed in revitalizing operations. With a small staff, procedural changes or new incentives and rewards may bear fruit quickly. In large organizations such as donor agencies, however, major change is much more complicated. This is due to a variety of reasons, which normally include the presence of entrenched bureaucratic systems; incentives and reward structures that may be difficult to change; resistance from parts of the organization that have benefited from the old way of doing things; opposition from the board of directors or governance structure; and organizational policies and rules established in an earlier time in different circumstances. In such complex organizations, changes in one area may not succeed because of lack of change elsewhere in the organization, or changes in certain areas may invite a backlash from other parts of the organization that are wedded to the old ways. If priorities are not reordered to incorporate the new vision, the new ideas may simply be added on to staff already burdened by full workloads, with no incentives to adopt the new thinking.

In complex organizations, *systemic* change must occur to revitalize or transform the institution. In such a systems change, several organizational elements are involved. These include:

- Leadership, vision and strategy. Leaders with clear vision are important in such a process. But a new vision can only be adopted if a strategy is developed to ensure its implementation.
- Organizational procedures and behaviour. Old procedures and systems must be altered to fit the new vision, otherwise work will continue to be done as in the past. Incentives to take up the new thinking and rewards for doing so are also essential to change behaviour. Staff may need training in new methodologies, and new staff with different skills may need to be hired. Resources will probably need to be allocated for these changes.
- Monitoring and evaluation systems. Regular monitoring of the change process is essential to ensure that progress is occurring and necessary corrections are made.
- Relationship to environmental forces. Since external factors are normally part of the motivation for change, reforms or innovations undertaken need to be viewed in relationship to the external environment and to the factors close to the organization that promoted the change initially. This involves going beyond incremental planning at the top to more participation and strategic organizational management.

ANALYSIS OF CHANGE AT THE WORLD BANK AND USAID

We now turn to a review of the World Bank and USAID to determine the extent to which these organizations have succeeded in adopting reforms and innovations in their organizational systems to incorporate the participation of the poor. The experiences of these two organizations will be reviewed against typical key indicators of successful organizational change. Given that the Bank and USAID are public institutions, one must use flexibility in applying organization change theory to their operations. For example, the governance structures of these two organizations are different in their composition, vested interests and political behaviour from those of a typical board of directors of a private corporation or a non-profit organization. Moreover, both the Bank and USAID are sometimes limited in changes they can make to their systems and procedures. In the case of the Bank, this stems from the way it is governed. USAID's limitations derive from the fact that it is a government agency subject to many uniform regulations that it does not have the legal or administrative authority to change.[1]

Leadership and Vision

Any organizational change that successfully incorporates a significant new direction requires leadership at the top – by the chief executive officer, most especially, and ideally including senior managers and the board. What is now recognized as essential in a leader is the ability to promote the new vision and values the organization wishes to espouse. 'Walking the talk' means that rhetoric alone is insufficient. In addition to articulating the new vision, a true leader will undertake organizational changes to support it and demonstrate the new behaviour expected throughout the organization.

The World Bank

James Wolfensohn, president of the World Bank, has provided strong leadership at the World Bank in regard to the participation of the poor. Immediately upon his arrival in June 1995, he began to do things differently. Right away, he started travelling to borrower countries. By November 1996, 18 months later, he had been to 28 client countries (Blustein, 1996). In each country, he met with NGO and CSO representatives, many of whom had been critical of the World Bank's practices for several years. This was a first for Bank presidents. He listened to their concerns and promised a new day of dialogue at the Bank. He went into poor communities and villages, sat with chiefs and elders and listened to them describe their concerns. He explained the work of the organization as a fundamental human enterprise to make people's lives better. He declared that it had to get along with NGOs and other critics, all of whom should be working together in the development enterprise. In short, he began to create a new vision for the Bank and new norms of behaviour for its leaders (see Chapter 2).

USAID

Shortly after being appointed USAID administrator by US President Clinton in 1993, Brian Atwood announced a total reform of the agency. The reform was intended to

> *reorient all its operating and management systems away from the imperatives of a traditional bureaucracy and base them on participatory planning, consensus among partners around a development hypothesis, greater trans-*

> *parency and flexibility, and increased teamwork and decentralization of authority.* (La Voy and Charles, 1998)

Atwood hired a senior policy advisor for participation almost immediately, an important indication of his interest in this topic. Four months later, he issued a statement of principles on participatory development. The statement included ten principles that committed the agency to inclusion of the poor in both the formulation of development policy as well as individual project development. The paper stated that 'Development assistance works best when it contributes to efforts that people in the recipient society are already attempting to carry out, and when it fully takes into account the priorities and values of affected groups' (Atwood, 1993). It was a clear and bold commitment by the agency, and signalled a new path for an organization that had been almost rudderless for several years prior to his arrival.

In regard to engagement with NGOs, Atwood reached out to consult with both US and Southern NGOs in a way unprecedented for USAID. He set the tone for agency staff to follow suit in consulting with NGOs on a wide variety of topics and in the design stages of new initiatives. NGOs, in turn, assisted the agency in their efforts to reach out to the poor for involvement in policy formulation and project design.

Both leaders have continued throughout their tenure to set a high moral tone and to admonish agency staff to put into practice the most fundamental of development principles: to engage the poor in the decisions concerning interventions designed to help them.

Leadership at Lower Levels

Although the Chiefs of both the World Bank and USAID have provided significant leadership regarding participation of the poor, behaviour of senior managers at lower levels shows a decidedly mixed picture.

The World Bank
Prior to Wolfensohn's arrival, from 1988 through 1995, the World Bank had only a few senior staff who were proponents of participation. Two who stand out were Moeen Qureshi and Sven Sandstrom. Qureshi, while senior vice president of operations, agreed in 1989 to create the learning group on participation. According to a former Bank staff member interviewed in 1998, he did so in spite of opposition to the idea by all regional vice presidents and sectoral managers.

Sandstrom, while a managing director, took a leadership role in promoting participation during the days of the learning group. At its midpoint, he urged changes in the operation of the group to make its work more widely accessible to Bank staff.

Robert Picciotto, head of budget and planning in the learning group's day and now Director General of OED, coined the phrase 'the iron triangle', meaning engagement of the Bank, the government and the people. He noted that unless the Bank and the recipient government involved the poor in the planning of initiatives intended to benefit them, such efforts would not be successful. He also has been an innovator and has developed processes to create more flexibility and promote recipient government ownership in Bank-funded projects.

Ismail Serageldin, who had been one of the most enthusiastic members of the NGO–Bank Committee in the late 1980s (see Chapter 2) focused a good deal of attention on NGO concerns including participation when he became vice president of environmentally and socially sustainable development.

Since Wolfensohn's arrival, no one among the vice presidents, managing directors or other senior managers, other than those mentioned, has been a champion of participation.

Even though the president has been tenacious in spelling out the new vision for his agency, he has not yet succeeded in convincing his staff – especially his senior staff – that participation of the poor is essential to the Bank's success. For the most part, staff simply do not see participation as a strategic issue.

USAID

USAID's experience in regard to its senior managers reveals a more complex picture. One major reason for the complexity is that at the same time as the internal reforms were being undertaken, many in the US Congress were vigorously trying to shut down the agency and reduce or even eliminate the foreign aid programme. The Congressional attack had been unforeseen and absorbed significant time of the assistant administrators and senior staff between 1995 and 1997. In a stocktaking of reforms held in 1998, USAID described the problem this way:

> *The reform effort had encountered some daunting obstacles. These included changes in Congress, drastic budgetary reductions, a morale-devastating 'reduction in force', and – perhaps costliest of all – the compelling demands upon most of the Assistant Administrators and senior staff, which had precluded their coalescing around an Agency-wide management plan to implement the*

> *reforms. The lack of attention to leading the reform effort, in turn, left those units and individuals that had most fully adopted the new approaches unsupported when their innovations collided with the 'business as usual' of their bureaus or supervisors* (La Voy and Charles, 1998)

Beyond this group, there were a variety of attitudes expressed by other senior managers and long-time employees towards the reform effort. One group of very sceptical long-time employees saw the reforms as yet another 'fad' that would consume their time, but then fade away. A second group was interested in the reforms, but also feared efforts would probably amount to nothing. Yet a third group, which included mission directors and senior staff in many countries as well as headquarters staff, was enthusiastic about the reforms, worked vigorously to implement them and continue to do so today.

Strategy

For any major change, a strategy is essential to translate the new vision into reality for the organization. The incentives, human resource issues, changes in systems and procedures all form part of the strategy. The most important function of a strategy, however, is to convince the staff of the organization that the changes about to be made are necessary to enhance its ability to meet its goals.

The World Bank

From the time that the World Bank was created in 1944 until the 1980s, its mission was clear. It was a bank whose purpose was to make loans to client countries and to ensure repayment, with a broad goal of promoting economic growth in developing countries. During the 1980s, in addition to the advocacy by environmental activists, the Working Group and others both inside and outside the Bank began urging it to pay more attention to alleviating poverty. By 1990, the organization announced that its major objective would be poverty reduction. For a lending institution focused on economic growth to make the changes necessary to redirect its energy to reducing poverty was, and continues to be, a challenging task. The resulting ambivalence about these often conflicting goals is at the root of many of the Bank's problems as an institution.

The Learning Group's report, which was approved by the Board in September 1994, included an action plan to incorporate participation throughout the institution. The plan included a variety of innovations and reforms to support mainstreaming efforts (see Chapter 2).

Given the broad scope and detail of the action plan, hopes for participation were high in early 1995. However:

> *By 1997, the momentum appeared to subside. The IGP ceased meeting. The Bank discontinued the quarterly 'flagship' progress reports. The senior management committee overseeing the implementation of the participation action plan disbanded after its chairman left the Bank. The system of regional participation of focal persons faded away. When the central participation coordinator moved to another position, he was not replaced for more than a year. He had been critical in fostering quality control in the regional participation action plans. The Bank terminated funding for the FIAHS. In essence, the Bank declared victory and moved on. Many of the most important institutional structures, processes, and incentives for promoting participation were allowed to disappear. No one could say if participation had indeed become mainstreamed. The progress report was postponed from 1998 to 2000. (Van Wicklin, 1998)*

As described later in this chapter, by 1998, Bank staff were still calling for evidence to prove the value of participation. Incentives to reward participation by staff were not in place. Although the Strategic Compact – the Bank's major reorganization that took effect in 1997 – allocated US$10 million in incremental resources to the regions to support participation and social assessment, many Bank staff felt they had less money to work with (Aycrigg, 1998). Many felt this money was being used for other things, depending on the desires of country department directors. Adequate monitoring had not been done, so no reliable data was available to show whether participation had been incorporated.

Perhaps more than anything else, the failure to define participation of the poor as a strategic necessity to achieve its goal of poverty reduction explains why participation has not been widely promoted within it.

USAID

USAID's reform, which started in 1993, was part of a government-wide undertaking to 're-invent government' through application of the Results Act. This Act was intended to apply to government private sector practices of linking agency operations directly to results. The same year the Results Act was made law, US Vice President Albert

Gore undertook a national performance review intended to stream-line government and explain its value more clearly to the general public. The USAID administrator Brian Atwood declared that the agency would be a 'reinvention lab' to pioneer the effort launched by the vice president (La Voy and Charles, 1998).

A central tenet of the government-wide reinvention effort was that an organization identifies (and listens to) its customers and holds itself accountable for results that the customers value. USAID identi-fied as its customers the people of developing and transitional countries who are end-users or beneficiaries of USAID programmes: that is, primary stakeholders.

From that vantage point, it undertook an agency-wide transforma-tion to reorient itself from a hierarchical bureaucracy to an organization that undertook participatory planning, built consensus among its partners on development hypotheses and – through the use of teamwork and decentralized authority – worked towards achieving results in a transparent and flexible way. Although USAID's transfor-mation originated with the Results Act and Brian Atwood's arrival as administrator, the results approach did have some antecedents inside the agency. For example, the assistant administrator for Latin America and the Caribbean in the years immediately preceding Atwood's arrival had promoted a results management approach. When the reforms were instituted, this approach was adopted throughout the agency.

How well has USAID succeeded in making this transformation? Elements of USAID's strategy included incentives, human resource issues and changes in systems and procedures, for example. As with the Bank, USAID encountered a significant number of 'roadblocks' in its reform effort, but from the beginning, USAID, unlike the Bank, defined participation of the poor as an essential part of the strategy to achieve its goals.

Incentives and Rewards

Organization change theory consistently states that appropriate incentives and rewards for staff need to be instituted in order to promote desired new behaviours. If rhetoric changes but the incentive and reward structure does not, most staff will not change their behav-iour. Indeed, it is unrealistic to expect them to if they want to advance within the organization.

The World Bank

Traditionally, the basic incentives and rewards of the Bank have focused on staff being successful in 'moving money' – formulating, preparing and bringing loan proposals before the Bank's board for approval, and getting money disbursed to the borrowers. This practice is what staff call the Bank's 'approval culture'. In the days when it defined itself exclusively as a lending institution, such incentives and rewards made sense. Work was done according to a particular schedule based largely on economic factors and bureaucratic requirements.

Ever since the days of the Bank's learning group on participation, changes in incentives and rewards have been repeatedly called for. Below is a chronology of the calls for changes in incentives and rewards.

At the February 1992 workshop on participation midway through the learning group's work, the need for changes in incentives and rewards was discussed. The workshop report noted the following:

> *Some Bank participants felt that career advancement and salary review depend on bringing in projects to the Bank's Board. Only the exceptional staff member risks slowing down or experimenting and deviating from traditional project designs...There was an appeal to review the prevailing incentive structure that affects how the Bank is perceived, whom it recruits, and what kinds of risks are rewarded.* (Bhatnagar and Williams, 1992)

In the learning group's 1994 final report, a specific section on incentives was included in the action plan approved by the Board:

> *Stronger incentives. Attention to the participatory elements of operational work will be built into performance and promotion criteria. Staff who take particularly creative participatory initiative will be recognized, and the lessons learned from such projects and experiences will be disseminated broadly, as is already beginning to occur. The competencies for operational career streams will be reviewed and refined to include specific reference to the skills most relevant to participatory development.* (World Bank, 1994b)

The Bank report, written in preparation for the November 1998 Participation Conference, focuses again on incentives:

> *Among the most serious institutional constraints identified by Bank staff were the unevenness of support for participation at the management level, the limited resources available for participation activities, and contin-*

> *uing skepticism about the value-added of participation,*
> *given the lack of verifiable indicators ... Some staff report*
> *feeling the need to meet lending targets. This is reflected*
> *even at the project level.* (Aycrigg, 1998)

At the November 1998 participation conference, Rajesh Tandon had this to say in his synthesis:

> *We believe that specific incentives need to be built in for*
> *monitoring and rewarding staff performance in interna-*
> *tional agencies related to promoting and mainstreaming*
> *participation of primary stakeholders. In institutions like*
> *the Bank or other bilateral agencies, there has been in the*
> *past a tradition of rewarding people for moving big*
> *dollars. There has emerged a culture of individual entre-*
> *preneurship. We want to suggest that team work,*
> *listening, patience and the process of enabling participa-*
> *tion by hitherto excluded groups are new ways of*
> *behaving as task managers and those ways can only be*
> *developed and systematized if there are specific perfor-*
> *mance indicators and incentives and reward systems*
> *associated with that.* (Tandon, 1998b)

Shortly after these remarks, the president addressed incentives in this way:

> *On the question of incentives, that is, of course, central.*
> *It engages us at many levels. First, in changing the culture*
> *and then convincing people that, as part of that cultural*
> *change, there are rewards and there is support for change*
> *towards a participatory environment... There is the need*
> *for change, and what we have to do, quite clearly, is to*
> *reward and support the people that are moving in a*
> *participatory manner and try and educate the others,*
> *either with incentives or with recognition that they're not*
> *doing well and replace them.*

Some Bank staff argue that the changes in the Bank's personnel evaluation system do include incentives for participation. They point to the fact that managers are now assessed on the basis of whether they practice teamwork and have a client orientation in addition to more traditional Bank values such as appropriate knowledge and a drive for results. This is done through a '360-degree' personnel evaluation that includes ratings on the employee by peers, customers, supervisees and supervisor.

Although changes in incentives and rewards, on their own, will not produce organizational change, it is clear that without them, change will be much more difficult. In the case of the Bank, all indications appear to be that the predominant incentive for advancement and salary increases continues to be getting loan proposals prepared and approved and getting money disbursed to client governments. The promotion of participation continues to be done by those who are personally committed to such work or who are encouraged by supervisors who believe in it.

USAID

At USAID, changes in incentives and rewards were made in the early days of the reform effort. Several 're-engineering' teams redefined the core values of the organization in order to transform it from a 'fragmented hierarchy' to a more 'seamless' structure that focused on desired outcomes and allowed greater flexibility in achieving them. The five core values identified were:

- customer focus (rather than letting internal procedures define purposes and constrain performance);
- management for results (rather than by inputs);
- participation and teamwork (with partners, customers, and also within the agency);
- empowerment and accountability (giving teams the necessary authority and holding them accountable for results); and
- diversity (valuing and appreciating the differences all employees bring to the workplace, while ensuring inclusion for all employees at all levels within the agency) (La Voy and Charles, 1998).

Supervision and leadership were to be geared towards whether the agreed-upon objectives and intermediate results were being achieved, rather than on how a set of project activities was being implemented.

In 1996, the 360-degree personnel evaluation was instituted. Moreover, USAID endeavoured to make job classifications and rules for promotion 'supportive of high performance teamwork rather than only individual achievement' (La Voy and Charles, 1998).

In spite of these impressive efforts, the changes in incentives and rewards do not appear to have resulted in the pervasive change desired. One of the reasons for this may be problems associated with moving from a hierarchy to a team-based approach. The stocktaking done in 1998 produced the following comments:

Teamwork was not well understood, and teams that tried to incorporate all the necessary USAID players and had made decisions with extensive customer or partner engagement were, like any units in a traditional organization, subject to bureaucratic second-guessing, delays and reversals. (La Voy and Charles, 1998)

The use of teamwork at the bottom of an administrative hierarchy [USAID's strategic objective teams] is problematic when supervisors and leaders lack the experience of teamwork and underestimate the consequences of overturning team decisions or withholding authority. This can seriously damage morale and undercut the credibility of the reform effort. (La Voy and Charles, 1998)

As of late 1998, the agency was once again developing new precepts for promotion and revising agency awards and incentives to align these instruments with the new values and policies.

At USAID, in spite of efforts to change incentives and rewards, the lack of change on the part of some senior managers, their continued use of hierarchical decision making, and apparent disregard for new team-based work appear to have hindered change. One of the lessons noted in a paper on reform said: 'Teams are fundamentally different entities than offices, and they can be rendered ineffective by inappropriate management. We need to encourage use of teams at higher levels in the organization both to improve efficiency and broaden experience with this structure within the Agency.' (USAID, 1999).

Human Resources Development

Effective organizational change requires attention to human resources including recruitment of staff with new skills, training to carry out new procedures and training to raise awareness and build commitment to them.

The World Bank
The record in the Bank shows a mixed picture. At the time participation first became an issue to be studied, the vast majority of staff were economists with very little orientation towards or appreciation for the value of the other social sciences such as anthropology or sociology. In addition, few had skills essential for participatory work. The 1994 Participation Report identified the need to redress the 'skills mix' so that those with appropriate training and skills could be recruited into the Bank to carry forward the participation agenda.

Following the adoption of the Strategic Compact, money was made available to hire more social scientists.

> *As of September 1998, the Social Development Family had 169 staff including 118 in the regions, 32 in the anchor, and 19 in other sections of the Bank. Of these staff, about three-quarters are social scientists (including economists) and one-quarter are trained in other areas.* (Aycrigg, 1998)

This has helped to augment the efforts to carry out design and implementation of projects and policy development processes in a participatory way. Many of the social scientists hired into the Bank are academics interested in research and analysis, however. These professionals do not necessarily have the practical experience and skills essential for success in carrying out participatory work.

A second, largely unsuccessful effort has been training of key Bank staff to improve their skills in participation. In most cases, task managers and other supervisory staff who work on projects have mainly claimed to be too busy to attend such workshops. Rather, participants have been staff and consultants already convinced of the value of participation.

What has been successful in the Bank has been a noticeable shift in attitude of staff away from seeing themselves as 'experts' bringing solutions to problems of the poor. Many staff now understand that each project or policy development process must be viewed through the particular culture, geography, economic factors, and social organization. What is also better understood, according to a staff member interviewed in 1998, is that primary stakeholders' feelings, attitudes and beliefs have a profound effect on their willingness to use new services or new technology, and to be willing to take responsibility for and maintain such services or equipment in the future (pers com). Along with this change in attitude has come a certain humility and appreciation among some Bank staff that they have a lot to learn about development from primary stakeholders, themselves, as well as from other development practitioners.

USAID

At USAID, the mix of skills present at the time of the reorganization and attitudes towards development were significantly different from those of the Bank. USAID has had a rich mix of disciplines on its staff for many years. Moreover, the agency has had a long history of being an organization where much of its authority resides with staff living and working in developing countries, and where many of its employees are nationals of the countries it serves. Many staff had been involved in participatory efforts for several years (although it is safe to say that many such efforts did not systematically include the poor in decision-making roles in project identification and design).

Several innovations were undertaken to help promote participation in the agency:

1 *The Participation Forum.* From early 1994 until the middle of 1997, 23 sessions were held. The sessions, which generally included ample time for questions and discussions, were intended to raise awareness of how principles of participation have contributed to effective programmes across a wide spectrum of development challenges. Summaries were distributed to a self-selected 'participation network' numbering nearly 900 staff, and made available outside the agency.

2 *Participatory Practices Series.* This activity is a series of case studies that describe experiences of participatory practices. An example: *Engaging Customers in Activity Design: Democracy Partnership in Bangladesh.* Bangladeshi employees, from specialists to secretaries and drivers, learn new 'listening' skills, and conduct extensive rapid appraisal across the country; as a result, the direction of USAID's democracy programme is radically reoriented towards priorities voiced by poor women and men.

3 *Participation Working Group.* This group functioned during the first year and a half of the reform effort. It served as a vehicle for staff to voice concerns about the participation initiative and provided two-way communication on management issues affecting participation.

4 *Country Experiment Laboratories.* These were undertaken voluntarily in ten USAID missions in developing countries as the new operating system was being developed. Staff applied the new approaches to some or all of the mission's operations, and in so doing, demonstrated benefits of the reform approach, while serving as 'seed-beds of innovation and learning'. Staff using participatory methods found them to be rich sources of practical advice (La Voy and Charles, 1998).

The focus of these various efforts shifted as the reform process moved forward. The initial goal of these activities was to raise people's awareness of participation, increase knowledge of what could be done, reinforce staff's best instincts, and help to ensure that the value was integrated into the reforms of the operating systems. However, as problems arose with the reforms, these mechanisms provided important two-way channels for communication. Senior managers were able to hear and address problems impeding participation.

In a stocktaking of reforms conducted by USAID in 1998, the following finding was noted:

> *These challenges call for staff and partners to use knowledge and skills that may be new to them. Severe shortage of operating expense resources for training and resources for skilled facilitators – such as USAID has experienced in recent years – poses a serious obstacle to more rapid expansion in our use of participatory methods.* (La Voy and Charles, 1998)

In the same paper, USAID includes the following statement as one of seven major lessons learned about how to incorporate participation of the poor:

> *Lesson Six. Serious change requires major investment in training of both staff and partners. Changes of the sort that USAID has set out for itself require that employees and partners internalize the core values and how they apply to Agency operations. Effective teamwork requires that team members – as well as senior managers – understand their new roles in getting work done efficiently in a team setting. New ways of thinking must be learned that focus on strategies and tactics for achieving results that matter to customers, rather than on elaborate project planning. New operating procedures need to be learned, with new (and streamlined) documentation requirements. Presenting development hypotheses to relate intended intermediate results and strategic objectives involves new skills, as does defining measurable indicators and engaging customers and partners in the monitoring.* (La Voy and Charles, 1998)

In both the World Bank and USAID, human resource development efforts have produced important attitude changes but these have not resulted in widespread participatory operations. Insufficient training, or training that has not reached key people, have both been problems in these agencies.

Resources

In order to incorporate participation into the work of the World Bank and USAID, new resources were necessary for recruitment, training and instituting new procedures.

The World Bank

During the life of the Bank's learning group on participation, special resources were made available to task managers of selected projects to use in experimenting with participatory methods. In the two-year period immediately following the Board approval of the 1994 Participation Report, special funds were made available through the FIAHS, which provided over US$4 million during a three-year period[2] to incorporate participation processes into the design of projects. Other than these special funds, no regular budget money was made available for participation work. Thus, although the term *mainstreaming* was being used throughout the Bank to describe efforts to incorporate participation into its practice, money to hire new consultants or to hold special consultations or conduct surveys was not included in the regular budgeting processes of the organization.

In 1997, with the reorganization of the Bank, the FIAHS was eliminated. It was explained at the time that the Strategic Compact (the 'blueprint' for the reorganization) incorporated funds in each country department that *could* be made available for participatory processes, if seen as necessary and desirable by country department directors or task managers in charge of projects or policy development. In the opinion of many Bank staff, if managers are sympathetic to participation, funds are made available for such processes; otherwise, not.

As with incentives and rewards, in major reports written about progress incorporating participation in the Bank, the fact that resources have not been made available in any systematic way has been highlighted as a constraint to promoting participation within the organization. In the report prepared by the Bank for the November 1998 Participation Conference, the limited resources available for participation activities was noted by staff as one of the most serious institutional constraints (Aycrigg, 1998).

USAID

At USAID, although there was an organizational commitment made to overall reform by the administrator, the agency's resources were cut from outside. Less than two years after the start of the reforms, the US Congress made substantial cuts in its budget. Moreover, an internal agency decision made early in the reforms to create a new information management system (called the New Management System) ultimately cost US$100 million. These two factors forced a 'reduction in force' – personnel lay-offs, elimination of training programmes, and reductions in or elimination of development projects. Not surprisingly the energy of some senior staff was diverted away from the reforms.

The New Management System was a grand fiasco early on in the reform years. The desire was to create an information system that would provide data as soon as financial and programme decisions were made anywhere in the agency, so that they could be entered into the system and accessed immediately. This would enable the agency to track all its finances, and aggregate data on performance and costs of its programmes worldwide. Although software was ultimately developed and is being presently used at the agency headquarters, the problem of how to transfer data to and from agency missions was never resolved. Needless to say, this very expensive unsuccessful effort hindered implementation of change.

The agency now understands that resource constraints necessitate a certain 'pacing' of reform efforts so that staff understand what is being required and why. The coincidental timing of reforms, budget reductions, staff lay-offs, the New Management System and threats to the agency's existence created confusion and anxiety.

USAID noted in its 1998 stocktaking that 'it has vastly under-invested in staff and partner training, partly as a result of severe budget reductions' (La Voy and Charles, 1998). The agency has now recommitted itself to such training, however, even within the restrictions of its current budget. Examples are 'Reaching 4 Results' workshops that have taken place in various missions for both staff and implementing partners, and a management and leadership course given during 1999 and 2000.

Although USAID has increased training opportunities in spite of continued budget restrictions, the Bank's commitment of resources for participation continues to depend on the willingness of particular supervisors, rather than on any systematic allocation of budget.

Systems and Procedures

When an organization undertakes a fundamental change, the systems and procedures that supported the 'old' way of doing business are upgraded, changed or thrown out altogether. New methods take their place which support the new behaviour expected. In this regard, the World Bank and USAID present two different sets of experiences.

The World Bank

At the World Bank, in the first two years of implementation of the participation action plan, there were virtually no structural changes to ensure that participation actually occurred. Efforts were carried out within the framework of the 'old' organization. There were a few innovations, such as participation action plans in the regions and a senior oversight committee that was to review and monitor these plans and their implementation.

In 1997, with the adoption of the Strategic Compact, the Bank committed itself to a full restructuring in order to put more of its staff, resources and decision-making authority in the recipient countries. This was intended to make the Bank more responsive to recipient governments and better able to act and adapt to changing conditions. At headquarters, cross-disciplinary networks were created to serve the country departments with technical skills. Within one of these networks, the Social Development Department was created at headquarters to offer guidance on issues such as participation.

Moving more Bank staff and decision-making authority to recipient countries is sound for many reasons. It enables more consistent communication and engagement with the recipient government, greater ability by the organization to respond to changing circumstances, and greater understanding of the particular country. However, this does not mean that participation of the poor will be incorporated any more effectively into the procedures and systems of the Bank. In cases where its senior staff with an interest in participation are present, their influence can and does help to ensure that projects and policies developed in that country are done so in a participatory manner.

The one extant Bank database on participation indicates that the progress gained in numbers of projects that incorporated participation in the years 1995 and 1996 was lost in 1997 and 1998, the first two years following implementation of the Strategic Compact (Van Wicklin, 1998).

In the Bank's report prepared for the November 1998 Participation Conference, it states that 'the most important institutional constraint to mainstreaming participation in Bank-financed investments has been the cycle for identifying, preparing, implementing and monitoring projects' (Aycrigg, 1998).

The rigidity of the project cycle and the difficulties it poses for incorporating participation of the poor into project development have been well known since the early days of the Learning Group. Although the Learning Group's 1994 final report says little about it, the NGO addendum to the report makes a plea to change the project cycle to allow for participation of the poor.

In 1997, learning and innovation loans and adaptable lending instruments were introduced on a pilot basis to provide flexibility in terms of experimentation and to enable the client government to test approaches through pilot projects. They can also be quickly authorized by Bank management without waiting for the fully-fledged loan package to be approved by the Board. Neither of these innovations provides per se for the participation of the poor, however. According to Bank staff, whether such participation is included depends on how the instruments are managed. In one experience recounted in interviews in 1998 by a group of NGOs in a Central American country, the speed with which one adaptable loan was approved meant that there was insufficient time for interested NGOs to get information about the intended project from the project information document and to have input into the formulation or design of the proposed intervention (pers com).

The more general issue of time required to do participatory project formulation and design has not been adequately addressed. Repeatedly, it becomes a problem in meeting deadlines associated with the project cycle. This is an issue (along with incentives and rewards, training and resources) that has been highlighted as a problem since the days of the learning group. Many Bank staff say that although participation is one of several good things to do, they simply haven't the time, incentives or training to undertake it.

USAID

USAID has carried out a comprehensive reorientation of its systems and procedures to enable it to put in place a 'results-oriented' process of designing and implementing its projects and policy reform efforts. Participation of the poor is one of the central tenets of this reform. The reorganization has affected all aspects of the agency's framework, from procurement regulations to policy and project formulation to its monitoring and evaluation systems.

The USAID reorganization has had plenty of problems to solve, but it represents a total commitment to reshaping its orientation. As described in USAID's paper prepared for the November 1998 Participation Conference:

> *It undertook to reorient all its operating and management systems away from the imperatives of a traditional bureaucracy and base them on participatory planning, consensus among partners around a development hypothesis, greater transparency and flexibility, and increased teamwork and decentralization of authority.* (La Voy and Charles, 1998)

The agency reorganized all its decisions, resources and activities around particular 'strategic objectives' or significant development results. These objectives are developed collaboratively by staff, and sometimes partner representatives and customers, in expanded teams. Once determined, particular intermediate results and indicators of intermediate results are agreed upon.

A USAID staff member directly involved in the reforms from the beginning, initially in a country mission and later at headquarters, had this to say about this change:

> *[Strategic Objective] teams, and the concept of teamwork more generally is a potentially powerful tool in breaking down institutional barriers both within USAID and between USAID and other institutions. Establishing such teams is a very effective way to promote more participatory values, behaviours and processes. In my mind, this was one of the more radical organizational changes introduced in the Atwood era reforms. How well this approach is working has not been assessed in any systematic manner yet.*

For the most part, the expanded strategic objective teams involve host government officials, other donors, US NGOs and contractors that are implementing USAID programmes. In some instances, representatives of the poor are involved. The importance of these teams to participation seems to be in setting an example by seeking a variety of inputs from outside the agency into the design of development objectives and indicators of intermediate results. In most cases, the idea is not so much to engage large numbers of the poor in this process, but rather to show the value of seeking a variety of outside views. By modelling such behaviour, the agency hopes to encourage those involved to reach out more to the poor and secondary stakeholders with whom they work. USAID also continues to carry out participation efforts through the projects, themselves.

This new methodology brought with it new reporting systems and new bureaucratic behaviour. The USAID 1998 stocktaking describes it this way:

> *... An aspect of the reforms intended to increase the Agency's flexibility and ability to respond to customers – the focus on results – in practice led to cumbersome, overly-elaborate reporting systems and time taken away from listening to customers. Major corrections are*

> *currently being undertaken to realign the results manage-*
> *ment system.* (La Voy and Charles, 1998)

USAID also learned that streamlined directives that replaced the old regulations were not explained adequately to staff through training and written guidance. Therefore, many staff didn't understand required procedure. In fact, US NGO representatives, who had attended USAID meetings in Washington to learn about new regulations, sometimes found themselves later on explaining the new rules and procedures to USAID staff in developing countries. In the midst of so much organizational change, employees and partners need to know where to turn for authoritative answers on policy and for guidance and suggestions for how to approach unfamiliar new processes.

Since the 1998 stocktaking, the agency has made significant efforts to revise its Automated Directives System and it has consulted extensively with partners in doing so. The agency has also greatly expanded automated access to information regarding procedures, regulations, procurement and programmes through its website.

USAID, as a bilateral government agency, cannot change certain procurement and personnel regulations, budget 'earmarks' (money required by law to be spent on particular programmes) and certain delegations of authority that are uniform throughout all US government agencies. This places certain constraints on the agency's ability to change. Its *Reform Roadmap* noted the following lesson learned in this regard:

> *USAID is but part of a broader government structure.*
> *We often lack the authority to change externally imposed*
> *systems and processes... When facing these regulatory*
> *constraints, we need to be certain about which ones are*
> *real rather than imagined or internally created, and focus*
> *on those we can influence. At times this will mean*
> *communicating with external regulators and seeking*
> *relief.* (USAID, 1999)

This review shows decidedly different experiences at the World Bank and USAID. The Bank may have erred on the side of too little change in systems and procedures, whereas USAID perhaps erred on the side of too much, or perhaps too much too soon. At the Bank, although the Strategic Compact was instituted in early 1997 with a restructuring of the organization, the biggest impediment to participation – the project cycle – remains in place, albeit with limited pilot efforts underway in a few countries. USAID, after a total reorientation of systems and procedures, continues to make efforts to correct and refine these new tools five years after the reforms took effect.

Monitoring and Evaluation

Monitoring and evaluation are necessary in any organization and are all the more important when it undertakes change. Regular monitoring is necessary to judge progress, ensure that reforms are on track and to make any necessary corrections. After three to five years, an evaluation should be undertaken to determine whether the reforms have been fully implemented and to assess whether such changes have succeeded in helping the organization reach its goals more effectively.

The analysis of monitoring and evaluation systems shows clearly the differences in approach undertaken at the World Bank and USAID. Until 1996, participation was monitored poorly, and overall results and impacts of Bank work were not evaluated at all. In 1997, the Bank instituted the Strategic Compact, which significantly altered the way it does business, but it has not incorporated monitoring and evaluation of participation in a strategic way. Nor has it created an overall impact evaluation system. Therefore, although the organization has been functioning with its new structure for four years, its ability to measure results is no better than before the Strategic Compact took effect. It is only now that the Bank is recognizing the need for such changes.

USAID, on the other hand, boldly took on all organizational elements in its re-engineering, including measurement of results and impact. They have encountered serious problems in the processes they instituted to determine results. But, as they monitor the new systems, they continue to identify what is not working in order to take steps to correct it. With this commitment to adapt the new systems and procedures so that they work in favour of the agency's strategy and vision, they stand a much better chance of creating an organizational structure and set of practices that enable 'customer-driven' or participatory development. That enables measurement of results as well.

The World Bank

World Bank officials often say that if there were more evidence to show that benefits of participation by the poor outweighed costs, and that it contributed to project sustainability, there would be more support for its incorporation. The Bank's report prepared for the November 1998 Participation Conference included the following issue as one to deal with in the future:

> *It will be imperative to develop convincing evidence to demonstrate the value-added in terms of, for example, reduced risk, improved performance, and increased ownership. This will be the key to convincing governments that participation is an effective development strategy and to convincing Bank management to think of participation as an investment strategy.* (Aycrigg, 1998)

Similar statements on the need for evidence have been made since the early days of the Learning Group on Participation in 1990. This is notwithstanding the evidence produced by the Learning Group and later by other Bank staff on the positive correlation between participation of primary stakeholders and sustainability of project benefits, as well as the value of participation in formulation of development policies.

In spite of the continuously expressed desire for evidence, no adequate monitoring or evaluation systems have ever been established to determine the value of participation to sustainability of benefits, or the actual costs and benefits of participation in Bank-funded projects and policy development processes.

The Social Development Department database has recorded participation in Bank-funded projects since 1994 by analyzing project appraisal documents. Eight types of participation are recorded, six of which are the participatory mechanisms described in Chapter 3. Incorporation is determined by the number of projects defined as participatory and which of the six levels the projects contain.

> *This methodology is fraught with problems and highly unsatisfactory as a means of measuring the mainstreaming of participation. OED analyzed the data because it is the only existing database we identified with participation data covering 1994–98. The data can be used for indicative purposes only.* (Van Wicklin, 1998)

Van Wicklin's explanation of the weaknesses of this database illustrates the problems:

> *The Social Development Department's system of recording participation has several well-known limitations which need stating to qualify the analysis that follows. First, only if participation is mentioned in the appraisal document does it get recorded in the database. Second, because projects are scored only at the time of approval,*

*the database provides a static snapshot for only that
year's cohort of projects entering the portfolio, not a
dynamic analysis of the current state of participation in
the Bank's entire portfolio of projects under preparation
or implementation. It is not a live database. Third,
appraisal documents record intentions about participation in the implementation and evaluation phases, since
those phases are in the future at the time of appraisal.
These intentions may fail to materialize. Some participation specialists believe appraisal documents overstate the
likely amount of participation to actually take place.
Fourth, any participation at all counts and can apply to
any part of a project, so participation could be very
limited in terms of breadth, duration and other measures
of extent. In fact, sometimes the participation applies to
the side effect of a project, for example involuntary resettlement, and not the main project activity, for example,
the dam causing the involuntary resettlement. Fifth, the
mechanisms (or 'levels') of participation are so broad and
poorly defined that rank ordering them is difficult. For
example, empowerment includes 'strengthening financial
or legal status' and 'capacity building', which – though
useful – does not imply any greater control by stakeholders, while collaboration includes stakeholders being given
principal responsibility for implementation. Sixth, and
unconfirmed, is the possibility that using different coders
in different years has led to inconsistencies in how participation was recorded. The Social Development
Department itself states that the coders were inadequately
trained, there was no manual or codebook to guide the
scoring, that the process was not closely supervised, and
therefore urges extreme caution in using the data. While
the first five caveats could bias the data in absolute terms,
as long as the recording system is consistent, the data
would be indicative in relative terms, that is, useful for
comparisons between years, regions, sectors, project
phases, and other data contained in the database.* (Van
Wicklin, 1998)

Using this database for the evaluation leaves questions about the
validity of the information drawn from that database. More importantly, questions remain as to why the Bank did not put into place a
rigorous monitoring system when implementation of the action plan

began in 1995 – and when such a monitoring system will be created. The evaluation of results and impacts of projects are also inadequate. Until very recently, the Bank has operated on an 'audit' basis, measuring only whether all inputs and outputs have been accomplished. Implementation of Bank-financed projects can take as long as six years. The organization does not, however, review projects it funds at the ten-year point to determine if the project has had the impact intended. The president began pushing for a change to a 'results' orientation as early as 1996. At that time, he said, 'Moving from approval to results is not only important ... it's something institutionally we have to do – or we won't exist in 10 years' (Blustein, 1996). At the time of the November 1998 Participation Conference, the Bank was finally recognizing the need to begin measuring the results of its work in order to ascertain the impact of its interventions.

USAID

At USAID significant efforts have been made to transform the agency into one that focuses on results and impacts. At the time of Atwood's arrival, it was using the LOGFRAME system to plan projects (see Chapter 3). This system revolves around achieving the 'project purpose', which is a clear objectively verifiable statement of the results sought by the project. Some, but not all, projects were chosen to be evaluated for impact through the agency's Center for Development Information and Evaluation (CDIE).

The entire system of designing projects has now been changed to incorporate a monitoring framework for measuring progress towards results. New requirements are in place to carry out all work within the framework of a small number of strategic objectives:

> *Decisions, resources, and activities are all organized around accomplishing a given strategic objective, or significant development result. These are part of a strategy, developed collaboratively by USAID staff and partners in a given country and approved by USAID in Washington. Decisions about specific activities – how a given objective is to be accomplished – are made by the mission. The focus of supervision and leadership, therefore, is much less on how a set of approved activities (a 'project') is being implemented, but on whether the agreed-upon objectives and intermediate results are being achieved – and, if not, what changes might be required.*
> (La Voy and Charles, 1998)

USAID staff and contractors or grantees agree on certain intermediate results and indicators of those results to be used in annual reviews of project progress.

> The use of objectives, rather than sets of planned activities, permits flexibility that was not possible under USAID's previous operating system, which was defined by 'projects'. Not only is the field empowered to make changes as necessary without seeking Washington approval – and thereby respond more fluidly to customer priorities – but the focus is more consciously on learning. Achieving results is intended to be a learning process in which we take risks and learn from our mistakes; we use information about results to make modifications in what we are doing; and we share lessons learned with others inside and outside the organization. (La Voy and Charles, 1998)

Although headed in the right direction, this reform has sometimes brought with it a new bureaucratic rigidity with serious implications for development. For example, many USAID staff appear preoccupied with the semantics of strategic objectives, intermediate objectives and indicators. Grantees and contractors often express aggravation at what they see as unnecessary delays and objections to the ways in which these objectives and indicators are worded in proposals. One grantee dubbed the behaviour 'the idolatry of indicators'.

Additional serious problems arise through a new system USAID has instituted to tie a contractor's fees or 'profit' to attainment of yearly intermediate objectives – a system known as 'performance contracting' widely used in business. This can lead to poor development decisions on the part of contractors in order to collect their fees. It has also led to wrong development decisions by agency staff. According to an interview in 1998 with a member of staff, some staff have refused to fund initiatives known to be effective because it may have taken more than one or two years for measurable results to be achieved (pers com).

Since 1998, the agency has eliminated the practice of seeking a direct relationship between annual budget allocation and performance measures. Its assessment of the revised procedures in 1999, which included interviews of partner field offices, suggests that the revised approach is more reasonable.

Governance

For international donor agencies, as in any organization, governance (a board of directors, a parliament or a congress) influences their ability to change.

The World Bank

The World Bank's board of executive directors is composed of: the principal donors to the Bank, which are the Northern industrialized countries and Japan (Part One countries) each with one representative; and powerful recipient countries, (Part Two countries) each with one representative. The majority of Part Two countries are represented as groups. For example, there are two executive directors for all sub-Saharan African countries. Votes are weighted in proportion to the country's contribution to the Bank's capital. The executive directors represent the interest of their governments in deliberations at the Board level.

At times some directors support advocacy efforts of NGOs regarding reform. This occurred in the case of the Sardar Sarovar (Narmada) Dam in India where certain directors from both Northern and Southern countries ultimately agreed with Indian, other Asian and international NGOs who had waged a seven-year campaign to stop the dam. The Narmada project, which had environmental and resettlement problems from the beginning, had no informed public participation or proper access to information on the part of local people, NGOs or even Bank directors themselves! By the time of the last Board vote on the project in late 1992, six executive directors (43 percent of the vote) called for a suspension of the project (Udall, 1998).

Such alignment with NGOs is true more of the time for Northern directors who have often assisted NGOs in their advocacy efforts on information disclosure and gender, and the establishment of the inspection panel. This is so for a number of reasons. One is that the orientation towards an issue taken by the executive branch of the particular government (which chooses its executive director) may be the same as the NGOs' view. A second is that the personal beliefs of the director may coincide with those of the NGOs involved. And a third is that NGOs and their constituents, since they are voters, have influence in their countries' legislative bodies. The parliament or congress in some countries has oversight of the World Bank, and funding authority for its soft loan window, the IDA.

An example of the third point occurred in 1992 and 1993 when NGOs used the funding authority of the US Congress as a tool to promote adoption of a new information disclosure policy and the establishment of the inspection panel (see Chapter 2).

The above example of Narmada notwithstanding, the Bank's board generally was not supportive towards NGO efforts in the years 1983–1988 on information disclosure and accountability reforms. Most executive directors saw these as political efforts by 'radical' Northern NGOs that were not in the interests of recipient governments. However, the board became interested in the potential role of operational NGOs (Northern and Southern) as it emerged in project implementation because they saw such involvement as having the potential to make Bank-funded projects more effective through their links with the poor. Thus, in 1994, when the participation report of the Learning Group came before the board, with an action plan for incorporating participation into the Bank, the board approved it.

In spite of this support, in 1997, when the president asked the Board to prepare a proposal that would have allowed Bank management to make grants to NGOs for capacity building work with the poor, the board was adamantly opposed. Executive directors from Part One countries argued that it was the exclusive prerogative of the Board to make funding decisions. The Part Two directors indicated that such funding arrangements with NGOs should be left to the recipient governments to determine, and that recipient governments were, and should continue to be, the sole clients of the Bank (pers com, 1997). The board argued that any engagement with NGOs should be carried out by governments on a bilateral basis – with their 'own' NGOs. Recipient governments wanted to preserve their ability to decide which NGOs to fund, if any. This was probably due to the view of many recipients governments that some NGOs are actually political operators, or it was motivated by a desire to maintain as much funding control as possible over NGOs operating in their countries.

What may have added to the antagonism towards NGOs is the fact that rarely, if ever, do representatives of the Bank, the recipient government and NGOs meet together to discuss Bank-related issues. Traditionally, NGOs meet with either the Bank or the government. The missing party is often the scapegoat for some or all of the problems discussed.

Since the president's failed efforts on NGO grants, some notable progress has been made in the attitude of the Bank's board to NGOs, generally, and more specifically towards the participation of the poor. This is due to several factors. One is that members of the Working Group have now had three annual discussions with the full Board. It is clear through these efforts that each side feels increasingly comfortable with each other and wishes to communicate effectively about its concerns. Second, more Southern NGOs are making efforts to get to know their directors and to explore issues of common concern with them. Third, some of the cases in which NGOs and the poor have participated in consultations regarding the formulation of their country's assistance strategy may have begun to alter the attitudes of directors towards NGOs. In several instances, involvement of NGOs and other civil society organizations in consultations had 'direct, identifiable impacts on the CAS, primarily on policy formulation, strategy focus, and institutional capacity. For example, the primary focus of the Colombia CAS was changed to address issues of violence and public insecurity. In Madagascar the sense of exclusion felt by the coastal and minority population in the high plateaus was identified, leading to a stronger focus on partnership and decentralization in the CAS' (Aycrigg, 1998).

The Board's August 1998 decision to encourage country assistance strategy consultations with civil society and to provide more publicly available information once adopted indicates that the Bank and its board have seen the value of consultations with civil society and that more should be done to involve and share information with such participants. Authoritarian recipient governments will probably continue to be resistant to sharing information with their citizens and to involving them in policy development processes. However, it shows the positive influence the Bank can have with recipient governments when it is willing to work constructively with civil society organizations in participatory processes.

USAID

USAID employees often say that their most important stakeholders are the members of the US Congress! This is so because of the power of the Congress to approve each year the agency's operational plans, and to appropriate the money to carry out such plans – indeed to allow the agency to continue at all.

Traditionally, the development orientation of the US foreign aid programme has been hampered by two things. The first is the direct linkage of foreign aid with US foreign policy interests. Foreign aid is used by the executive branch of the government (the president and his administration) to carry out foreign policy objectives regardless of development considerations in the particular countries. The clearest example of this is that Israel receives fully one-half of the entire foreign aid budget (called the '150 account'). The second impediment, known as 'tied aid', legally requires USAID to hire US contractors and consultants, to 'buy American' hardware and fly US airlines for example. This is in order to channel as much of the programme's resources back to voters in districts of congressional representatives.

During the Cold War, a large part of the rationale for foreign aid was to 'win' friends for the United States and 'fight Communism'. Indeed, the Soviet Union did the same thing on its part. Anti-Communist support by the United States for dictators such as Mobutu in former Zaire and Doe in Liberia is well known. Since the end of the Cold War, foreign aid has become less and less popular in industrialized countries, and particularly in the United States. In the United States, the end of the Cold War, together with a more conservative, homeward-looking majority of elected representatives in the Congress since 1994 (many of whom do not even have passports) have meant an uphill battle by USAID for funding each year. Therefore, USAID has had to 'package' its programme in a way that will be attractive to congressional representatives who vote on it. (This is so in spite of the fact that less than half of one percent of the entire federal budget goes to relief and development efforts.) Therefore, when determining the agency's programme each year, the focus cannot only be the most effective development interventions to make. Rather, 'what will sell on The Hill' is equally important in getting the money appropriated. Of course, these factors are not mutually exclusive. But the political considerations can lead to distortions in an agency's programme that work against effective development approaches.

Another problem for USAID in regard to foreign aid is the issue of earmarks. Earmarks are specific sums of money that USAID must spend on certain initiatives, and are passed by Congress usually at the urging of citizens who want to ensure that their particular interests are met. This tactic is used by citizens for two main reasons:

1   to convince reluctant lawmakers to approve the foreign aid budget by 'earmarking' large sums of money to be spent on programmes against which congressional representatives would be reluctant to vote, for example, 'child survival' initiatives; and
2   when they are concerned that USAID – left to make decisions on its own – might not spend as much as they want it to on certain initiatives, such as micro-enterprise (which some people see as a fail-safe way to reduce poverty and enable development).

As noted earlier, in the years 1995 and 1996, there was an effort by conservative representatives in the US Congress to close down USAID and reduce or eliminate the foreign aid programme. The efforts required by USAID and supporters in the US NGO, higher education and contractor communities to argue against this effort consumed enormous amounts of time and energy. As a result attention was diverted from USAID's reform efforts, especially on the part of some senior managers who were struggling for its very survival.

The governance structures of donor institutions can retard or advance progress, depending on the political orientations or vested interests of countries represented, as in the case of the Bank's board, or the values, orientation and knowledge of individual politicians, as in the case of the US Congress. Change of such structures is usually a slow process. But exposure of Bank executive directors or members of a congress or parliament to the benefits to a country of participation by the poor can have a positive effect on their attitudes towards such change. This has been seen in the examples of participation in formulation of the country assistance strategy. Participation Conference participants recommended a vigorous policy dialogue with recipient states on the issue of participation and civil society. If the Bank is willing to promote this topic more actively with recipient governments, with an emphasis on potential benefits to the country, governments may become more open to participation, along with their executive directors.

Accountability

Accountability that incorporates organizational monitoring and evaluation also includes the broader need for a donor agency to be held accountable by the citizens of a country who are intended to benefit from initiatives it funds. This was a topic of considerable interest at the November 1998 Participation Conference and indicates the growing expectation by NGOs for donor institutions to share information fully, to be transparent about their actions and involvement with recipient governments and to be willing to be held accountable to affected citizens regarding projects and policies (Group Six, 1998).

We have already examined institutional monitoring and evaluation of participation efforts. Among the other important elements of accountability for international donor institutions are information disclosure, transparency regarding a donor agency's actions with a borrower or recipient government, and mechanisms for holding donors accountable to citizens regarding project results or adverse effects of projects.

The World Bank

For the past 15 years or more, the issue of information disclosure has been a priority advocacy issue for NGOs seeking reform at the World Bank. NGO advocacy led to reform of the information disclosure policy in 1993 and efforts towards a policy of complete information disclosure continue. Transparency in the organization's dealings with recipient countries has become another important advocacy issue within the past few years. Although some information about specific projects and certain strategies and policies related to economic and sector work is now being shared, the Bank's discussions and negotiations with recipient governments are carried out in virtual secrecy. Participants at the November 1998 Participation Conference were most eager to see its Consultative Group meetings regarding a particular recipient country held in the country rather than in a distant Northern capital (Group Six, 1998). It is at these meetings that the recipient government's representatives negotiate with the organization as to the total amount of Bank money to be committed for a particular year. Conference participants also called for participation of civil society representatives at such meetings in the future. Coverage of these meetings in the country by local media would also begin to open these up to scrutiny by the public.

The third element of accountability is the ability of citizens to hold a donor institution accountable for project results or related negative effects. In 1993, NGO advocacy led to the establishment by the Bank of an inspection panel as a way to give affected citizens redress over grievances related to Bank-funded projects in their countries (see Chapter 2). Although the establishment of the inspection panel was a major step forward in terms of its accountability to citizens of recipient countries, given how the organization has tried to limit its scope and functioning since then, full accountability is far from ensured. As with participation, there are no career incentives to encourage staff to promote environmental and social quality in projects or even to fully implement reform policies.

USAID

Neither information disclosure nor transparency has been a major source of conflict between NGOs and USAID in recent years. The United States has the Freedom of Information Act, a law that enables citizens to gain access to a variety of information from public agencies. Moreover, during the past five years of reform at USAID, the agency has shared information more freely with NGOs and other interested parties than in the past. In an effort to be transparent and to provide information easily and equitably to all those seeking it, the agency has made significant efforts to provide automated access to information on its regulations, procedures, procurement, programmes and plans through its web page. Similarly, the agency's work with recipient governments has been somewhat more open to scrutiny. In a few instances, NGOs, other civil society organizations, and the poor have been involved in USAID–recipient government planning regarding the donor's strategy for the country.

Regarding accountability, no effort has been promoted, either by the agency itself or by NGO advocates, to create anything similar to the inspection panel at the Bank. Such a mechanism is essential, however, for a donor agency to be fully accountable to its 'customers' – the poor – in recipient countries.

CONCLUSIONS AND LESSONS LEARNED

The World Bank and USAID have undertaken different ways of incorporating participation of the poor into their practices. The Bank chose an incremental approach, starting in 1994 – participation was one of several things some of its staff thought the agency should do – while USAID chose a strategic approach and transformed its whole method of operation – participation was seen as a key part of this new approach. Both organizations readily admit they have not succeeded but each has made substantial progress. What do these two case studies tell us about how best to incorporate participation of the poor in large donor institutions? What are the critical ingredients necessary for success in such an endeavour? The answers to these questions are embedded in the following lessons.

Lesson One

Leaders must promote and act on a clear vision of change.
In both organizations, strong leadership and vision at the top were in ample supply. Both leaders repeatedly articulated the need for change and the vision of more inclusive, participatory development as an important goal. President Wolfensohn's insistence that the Bank's work is a fundamental human endeavour intended to 'put a smile on a child's face' and Brian Atwood's emphasis on the need for USAID to 'listen to its customers' signalled that their visions were value-based. They emphasized that the changes in the two institutions were intended to produce a shift towards valuing the involvement of the poor and marginalized. Such messages broadened the framework of changes needed to involve not only intellectual or professional issues but also basic attitudes and emotions of agency staff. Their leadership set the tone for change in their agencies.

Lesson Two

Staff must be given the opportunity to influence, understand and accept changes that affect them.
The results of the two organizations' strategies present different pictures. One initially might assume that the transformational

approach undertaken at USAID would be the more successful approach. It involved the whole agency and clearly defined participation as essential to meeting its goals. The assessment in this book, however, shows that USAID has not made noticeably more progress than the Bank in its effort to incorporate participation into its practices. Although it undertook a total reform of its operations, systems, and procedures, USAID has encountered internal problems in implementing the reforms and formidable problems from the US Congress, which greatly complicated the task.

The Bank, for its part, did not take a strategic approach to incorporate participation. Although it had an action plan in 1994, the plan had no 'teeth' and lacked leadership and support among senior management. In spite of this, attitudes of many Bank staff have changed significantly. The organizational culture is moving away from an 'expert' approach and towards one that is more process-oriented, and open to incorporating into projects and policies views expressed by the poor.

What might account for these results? At the Bank, at the beginning of the work on participation, the vast majority of staff knew nothing about this topic. Almost all were economists and saw themselves as experts whose knowledge was the necessary ingredient to change economies in Southern countries. They had no understanding or appreciation for the value of participation of the poor. In fact, according to a Bank staff member who has been at the organization throughout the change process, those in the learning group were ridiculed as missionaries by other staff. Negative emails about the learning group's work were sent to try to stop their work. With time, however, and regular discussion and debate regarding participation of the poor, Bank staff have changed their attitudes significantly.

At USAID, on the other hand, the reform plan was announced from the top to staff around the world who already considered that their work included participation of the poor. Moreover, these staff had survived one poor leader after another over at least four years by ignoring changes made from headquarters and continuing with business as usual. Although Brian Atwood was welcomed as the administrator, his ideas for change were greeted with considerable scepticism by some although embraced by many others. Some were insulted that a participation policy was adopted and was being promoted, given their attitude that they were already running participatory programmes. Many USAID programmes had routinely incorporated the poor in project implementation, and to some extent in project formulation and design.

The contrast between the World Bank's approach and that of USAID is that the Bank was engaged in a *learning* process regarding participation, and USAID started its reform by *fiat*. USAID's reform was decided upon at the very top, and outside the agency through the Results Act. In the beginning, employees were not asked for input as to whether to reform; rather, they simply were presented with the decision to do so. Moreover, where insufficient training and orientation were given to explain the changes, employees felt they had little stake in the reforms. They lacked the opportunity to engage in the intellectual, emotional and behavioural reflection necessary to understand, and accept the changes.

Where efforts *were* made to help employees understand the reasons for reform, the response was more favourable. For example, in the Bolivia USAID mission, senior staff

> studied ... books to understand why corporations and public sector entities would want to take on such chaotic change. We also looked carefully at the track record of prior experience to see what results were actually achieved by others. Finally, we compared the approaches to reengineering described in the literature with that being taken by USAID. We then condensed this information and presented our findings to all Mission staff as part of the first overview briefing. Providing this information was extremely effective in neutralizing skepticism and promoting a positive 'let's try it' attitude. (Carduner, 1996)

In both agencies, staff had been rewarded for years for controlling the design and implementation of projects and policies based on their expertise as professionals. They were now being asked to give up control – at least partially. Such a change requires a fundamental shift in values and behaviour. Staff expected to make such changes have to be given the opportunity to explore what this means, what the consequences might be from such a different work approach, and whether they feel willing, able and equipped to make the changes. In order for an agency to use participatory methodologies in its work with clients and stakeholders, it needs to behave in a participatory manner with its own employees. This is what 'walk the talk' really means. The Bolivia case study again shows the value of addressing these fears directly and aiding people to work through them. Mission staff provided information and 'just in time' training (not more than two weeks before staff would be required to implement what was taught). 'We set about developing a six-month transition plan outlining specific steps that would be taken, including transfers of authorities and responsibilities. This exercise permitted us to deal directly with the fears related to lack of control ...' (Carduner, 1996).

Lesson Three

Fundamental change will be achieved only if structures and systems are altered appropriately.
The fundamental ingredients in this area are incentives and rewards, human resource development, resources, systems and procedures. Both the Bank and USAID have mixed records in these areas.

*   Incentives and rewards
    The Bank has not yet instituted specific incentives and rewards for participation, in spite of repeated calls for such changes. With the implementation of the Strategic Compact in 1997, however, changes that have taken place in the personnel system may encourage a positive attitude towards participation. The new personnel evaluation system includes several behavioural measures including teamwork, client orientation, a drive for results, and knowledge and learning. Discussions about values have become more important. Each region has done a values and mission statement; and the 'corporate day' in March 1999, which involved the president and all vice presidents and senior managers, had values as its theme.
    At USAID, the personnel evaluation system was altered in 1996 to reward teamwork and participation. These efforts did not, however, produce changes desired as rapidly as hoped for because of problems moving from a hierarchy to team-based operations. In late 1998, USAID made another effort to align personnel evaluations with the new values and policies.
*   Human resource development
    Records at the Bank and USAID show a mixed picture in this area. Since 1994, the Bank has hired a large number of social scientists to redress the balance with economists. Some staff think the executive management training carried out from 1997 to 1999 for 500 of the Bank's staff at Harvard University and elsewhere reinforced participation, openness to the poor and teamwork. Others disagree. In any case, the bulk of other training has not gone to key staff but rather to the already converted or long-term consultants.
    USAID readily admits its failure to invest adequately in training of staff and partners. This hampered employees in understanding their new roles, and using new operational proce-

dures appropriately. Since 1998, USAID has reinstated its training programmes.

- Resources

  Neither agency has invested adequate resources to incorporate participation of the poor in their operations. At the Bank, a special fund was available for participatory work from 1994 to 1996, but this was eliminated with the implementation of the Strategic Compact. Since then, many Bank staff have said availability of resources for participation depends on the interest of managers rather than systematic budget allocation.

  At USAID, the agency's budget was severely cut by the US Congress less than two years after the reforms were instituted, and a significant amount of money was wasted with the New Management System. These two events required personnel lay-offs and elimination of training as well as reductions in, or elimination of, development projects. Such budget reductions made implementation of the reforms much more challenging.

- Systems and procedures

  The Bank and USAID have had two quite different experiences in this regard. For the first two years of the participation action plan at the Bank, virtually no structural changes were made in the organization to accommodate participation. The Strategic Compact, launched in 1997, made some significant changes. Many staff, along with resources and decision-making authority, were moved from headquarters to recipient countries. The Social Development Department was created to provide guidance to country departments on participation and other social issues. The project cycle, however, which has been used for design and imple-mentation of projects for many years, has yet to be changed, and it continues to be viewed as the most important institutional constraint to incorporation of participation into Bank projects. On the other hand, the process used in developing the organiza-tion's policies, especially the country assistance strategy, has been altered in some instances to incorporate consultation with civil society.

  As for USAID, the agency undertook a total revamping of systems and procedures to change from a hierarchical orientation to a participatory, team-based and decentralized approach. While this represents an impressive undertaking, the agency initially failed to provide adequate guidance and training, although it has made significant efforts to correct these weaknesses in the past two years.

What can we draw from these two sets of experiences regarding the importance of procedural changes in a major change effort? The absence of procedural adaptations in the Bank's experience showed that a systems change was not underway. Participation was being allowed to seep into the work of the organization without benefit of incentives, rewards, adaptable procedures or adequate training. The president's vision incorporated participation, but, without an accompanying strategy, the vision alone did not convince Bank staff that participation would increase the institution's effectiveness or help reach its goal of reducing poverty.

At USAID, although a systems change was clearly underway, the fight with the US Congress over agency survival, as well as insufficient work on guidance and training in the new methodology, resulted in implementation problems. There continues to be significant support for the reforms and efforts to change continue.

From these experiences, it seems that organizational changes should be carried out in a particular order. The first change ought to be in the development of human resources, where involvement of staff in the design of the reforms, and subsequent orientation and training in the reforms undertaken are carried out. Once staff accept that such changes will assist the organization to reach its goals, they will be more open to instituting them. At that point, changes in the incentives and rewards structure could take place along with adaptations of the key procedures such as the way projects are designed and implemented.

Lesson Four

Systematically monitoring progress of major change is essential to achieving ultimate success.

The approaches undertaken by the Bank and USAID in monitoring and evaluating progress in change logically follow the basic orientation each has taken to reform. Since the Bank never adopted an organizational strategy to incorporate participation, no systematic monitoring or evaluation of participation work has been done. In 1999, it undertook an agency-wide evaluation of the extent of participation in its operations. What monitoring of participation mainstreaming has gone on has been carried out by NGOs or has been prompted by NGO questions.

At USAID, although the agency did not systematically monitor reforms during the first three years, in 1998, it did undertake a major 'stocktaking' to assess progress in the implementation and impact of the reforms. This was a serious effort, done in two stages, and involved input from 600 USAID staff and 300 USAID partners. Data were collected through review of documents, focus groups, individual interviews and surveys. This process provided the agency with significant input as to the progress made and the considerable challenges remaining to be overcome. Armed with this information, the agency subsequently began to make necessary corrections to keep the process of change on track. Monitoring has continued during the past two years, and additional adjustments have been made.

In both instances, essential monitoring information about change has been produced. In USAID's case, the agency, itself, generated these data. As for the Bank, in the absence of internal monitoring, NGOs carried out monitoring themselves, and repeatedly prodded the Bank until it provided such information. In these ways, such information was made available in both cases to reinforce efforts to incorporate participation. The Bank's own evaluation of participation undertaken in 1999 and 2000 is to provide information which can be used to make needed changes.

Lesson Five

Boards of directors must be aligned with the new vision, and the institutional changes needed to realize it.

Just as staff of donor agencies need to be convinced of the need for change, so also do those who govern the organization. Managers ignore them at their peril. If boards of directors are left uninformed, they may very well be resistant to reforms undertaken or reject them altogether, as they often have the power to do. At the Bank, executive directors were supportive of the Participation Action Plan in 1994 because they understood that such involvement could make Bank-funded projects more effective. Similarly, in several countries where participation of civil society has occurred in the formulation of country assistance strategies, executive directors from those countries have been enthusiastic if they have judged that such involvement helped lead to priorities that coincided with their governments' own interests.

In the case of USAID, among the members of the US Congress who wanted to close down the agency, some were ideologically opposed to foreign aid, or certain aspects of it, and will never be persuaded otherwise. But many were simply ignorant or misinformed about the foreign aid programme or even the proportion of the US budget devoted to it. When members of Congress learned from an NGO campaign that the entire US foreign aid programme was one per cent of the total US budget, and moreover, that only one-half of that went to relief and development, they voted to support the agency. More importantly, when USAID or its advocates could explain to congressional representatives what the agency's programmes actually did in terms of reducing poverty and improving people's lives, the legislators were most often persuaded to support the programme.

As has been the case with the Bank and USAID, a great deal can be done, not just by donor agency management, but also by interested outside pressure groups to educate and inform boards of directors about the value of instituting new methodologies such as participation of the poor.

In conclusion, these assessments show that both the Bank and USAID have made important strides in incorporating participation, using very different approaches. Now the stage is set for greater progress in this effort. Both agencies have learned important lessons, and there is momentum within each institution for further reform. Activists within the Bank and USAID – as well as the other donor agencies such as GTZ, DFID and Sida – have the opportunity to provide support and NGOs continue to apply pressure from the outside.

Chapter 5

Incorporating Participation of the Poor in Government Implementing Agencies

INTRODUCTION

Government implementing agencies in Southern countries are the 'frontlines' of development. As such, the development approaches they adopt largely determine how effective projects will be. Participation of the poor is far from the norm, and until government policies and operations are adapted, its incorporation will not be possible. The hierarchical way in which government implementing agencies are run comes not only from the the national government but also is caused by the hierarchical way donor organizations conduct their business and relate to recipient agencies through their funding programmes. Thus, efforts by recipient government organizations to change their ways are affected partly by their own systems and partly by the donors assisting them. Furthermore, because recipient government agencies depend to such a significant degree on donor funding, their orientation towards accountability traditionally has been to the funder rather than to the beneficiaries of development programs.

Since the 'development enterprise' began a half-century ago, little has been done to integrate participation of primary stakeholders into the work of government implementing agencies, and little has been available in development literature about the efforts that have been carried out. In recent years, however, more efforts are being made to integrate participatory methodologies into large public agencies in developing countries. There is still little written on the topic but it is increasing.

This chapter examines two major topics:

1   The first is an analysis of a favourable environment for national implementing agencies. This topic will be discussed in two ways. The first is by analysing the external influences on the environment imposed by bilateral and multilateral donors. The second is by analyzing internal factors in a country such as the political framework, efforts at decentralization and internal demands for greater citizen participation.
2   The second topic is the change a recipient government agency must undertake in order to promote participation of the poor. In this discussion, most of the categories used in Chapter 4 to examine reform in donor organizations will be used to analyse changes necessary in recipient government agencies. These include leadership, vision and strategy, organizational systems and procedures, behavioural change and training, resources and monitoring and evaluation. The chapter draws largely on data collected by the Working Group in its monitoring of World Bank projects, workshops held at the 1998 participation conference, and experiences described by Korten and Siy (1988).

BACKGROUND

Some borrower or recipient governments have begun to pay more attention to integrating participatory methodologies into their programmes. Reasons for this include the following:

*   efforts by international donors to stimulate their interest in participatory approaches;
*   acknowledgements of the failure of past approaches to development, which have not taken into consideration the local conditions, dynamics and particular circumstances of poor people; and
*   successful application of participatory approaches by NGOs and other non-profit organizations which have attracted the attention of government policy makers and planners (Thompson, 1995).

If more government bureaucracies are making efforts to integrate participatory methodologies into their project activities, why then are there so few accounts of these attempts in the development literature? Judith Tendler claims that 'the mainstream [development] donor community's advice about public-sector reform arises from a literature that looked mainly at poor performance' (Tendler, 1997). She goes on to say that

This means that countries and the experts that advise them have few models of good government that are grounded in these countries' own experiences. Second, and insofar as the mainstream development community has shown more interest recently in analysing good performance and 'best practice', it has focused too much on recommending that developing countries import ideas and practices from the already industrialized countries or from some of the more recently industrialized countries, particularly those of East Asia. (Tendler, 1997)

Antecedents of Developing Country Governments

The historical antecedents of developing country governments continue to influence present-day operations. They are important to acknowledge and understand as they are the roots of some of the current problems.

Colonialism

Just as Northern donor agencies are hampered in incorporating participation of the poor because of the way they were originally organized, so are recipient government implementing agencies constrained by the structures and procedures that have long been in place. Many developing countries were 'possessions' of colonial powers. Thus, their governments were set up as extensions of particular Northern powers, complete with bureaucratic procedures and cultural habits. Although systems in most countries have changed somewhat since independence, many of these countries retain at least some of the hierarchical structures instituted during the colonial era. Set up to serve a different government situated in a different culture, these systems are ill suited to the needs and norms of the particular country.

Family, Tribe or Ethnicity as Factors in Weak Government Agencies

Beyond the colonial heritage, many government ministries and agencies have informal systems that derive power from traditions of family, tribe or ethnicity. These systems provide access, advancement or entitlement based on family or ethnicity rather than merit, and serve as disincentives to behaviour geared towards the public interest or towards creating an environment in which a participatory development orientation can flourish.

In *Putting Theory and Practice to Work in Institutional Development: A Case Study and Analysis*, Neil Boyle analyzed a

World Bank project in Pakistan in which relationships among the public, the government bureaucracy and elected officials were predominantly based on ethnic, tribal or religious ties. These relationships had to be transformed in order for the participatory World Bank project to work (Boyle, 1998).

Non-Participatory Development Traditions

The way development assistance has been provided has perpetuated hierarchical ways of operating between donor and recipient country governments. This practice replicates the way in which donor agencies themselves are run, and is reflected in the ways projects and policies are designed and implemented.

In addition, the inherent 'charity' orientation of development assistance perpetuates certain hierarchical attitudes: providing money and human resources, but retaining control; budget and financial patterns determined more by the needs of the donor agency than by the recipient government ministry or its programmes; and preconceived solutions that the donor applies to problems in the recipient country. Many of these patterns began in the days when donors thought they were 'delivering' development solutions and have not changed.

In order to support the significant institutional and behavioural changes hoped for in developing country governments, donor agencies must change their own systems and practices used in their engagement with such governments. As DFID (formerly known as ODA) said in 1995, 'ODA itself has to practice the same principles of responsiveness, transparency and accountability with our aid recipient partners' (Feeney, 1998).

A FAVOURABLE ENVIRONMENT FOR A GOVERNMENT IMPLEMENTING AGENCY

As noted, our examination of a favourable environment for a government implementing agency will include an analysis of both external and internal influences. We focus our attention on the agency itself rather than on the national government, because significant change in a particular agency or large development project can take place if its particular environment is supportive of transformation even though the national government may not be. Most of the examples of the successful incorporation of participation of the poor in this chapter have occurred in agencies located in countries with authoritarian governments in power at the time of the change. This demonstrates that dramatic change can occur in spite of repressive national rule if relevant policies, laws and traditions are supportive of a role for local people.

A Changing Development Paradigm

External influences on government implementing agencies derive from both bilateral and multilateral donor organizations that have begun to change the way they view development. In recent years, development itself has been redefined. In earlier times, development was seen largely as technical intervention that would improve infrastructure, or economic performance, or provide skills needed to carry out programmes. Many development practitioners saw themselves as apolitical, and clearly differentiated what they did from political activity. More recently, however, those in the development community have come to understand that the very nature of development is political – not in a partisan way but in the generic sense of enabling people to assume more power over their lives and their economic and social circumstances. With this awareness comes the realization that development can no longer be carried out only as a technical intervention but must incorporate political and sociological aspects of the particular locality or region.

Donors now focus on issues of democracy and governance as legitimate aspects of an overall development programme. For example, since 1993 the USAID has incorporated work on both formal and informal democratic processes into its programmes in developing countries. This has involved extensive work to help develop electoral processes and strengthen political organizations. It has also included a focus on providing information, education and assistance to a wide variety of civil society organizations regarding their rights and responsibilities as citizens to enable them to become effective advocates for appropriate national and local development policies.

In the past four years, DFID has redefined its approach to development so as to incorporate an emphasis on human rights frameworks for achieving poverty reduction and participation, referred to as a 'rights-based approach'. Such an orientation examines how a donor can enhance the voice and influence of previously excluded groups. As Andrew Norton from DFID said at the November 1998 Participation Conference:

> *Alongside the commitment to participation, we need to put a thorough political and social analysis so a commitment to social justice and equity can be combined with that. Otherwise, there are dangers of vocal groups capturing benefits within those processes.* (Norton, 1998)

He went on to say that DFID:

> *is also investigating ideas of social accountability ... [we now recognize] that accountability to our development partners, including primary stakeholders is as important as accountability to the UK taxpayer, which is our traditional mode.* (Norton, 1998)

The World Bank, for its part, began in 1996 to focus on how to eliminate the 'cancer of corruption' (Wolfensohn, 1997). In 1997, it issued new guidelines to staff for dealing with corruption, and began working that year with six member countries to develop anticorruption programmes.

> *If a government is unwilling to take action despite the fact that the country's development objectives are undermined by corruption, then the Bank Group must curtail its level of support to that country. Corruption, by definition, is exclusive. It promotes the interests of the few over the many. We must fight it wherever we find it.* (Wolfensohn, 1997)

A third aspect of the changing development paradigm, which combines external and internal factors, concerns the roles played by different participants within a national context. Global events of the past 10 to 15 years, such as the end of East/West rivalry and a move away from command economies, have been part of the reason for this change. The growth of civil society is another. These factors, together with those at the national level such as widespread corruption, inefficiencies brought about by bureaucratic inertia, or prolonged conflict, have caused confusion in the delivery of basic services. Concomitant with this has been the continuing growth of multinational corporations and the globalization of the marketplace, making these corporations stronger than ever and able to function with relative ease across state boundaries. This situation has led to debates as to the roles of state and non-state participants and what the responsibilities of each should be within a national context. A new clear definition of the roles of government, civil society and business, and how each interacts with the others as they all contribute to the growth and development of a country, is needed for the modern era. Debates continue as to what constitutes the ideal and how these participants can most appropriately align with each other for maximum effectiveness.

At the same time as external forces are influencing national governments and the ways in which they operate, so also are internal forces at work to change relationships among those involved in development.

Political Framework

The existing political framework of a country or region can help or hinder participatory efforts. Sometimes the country's constitution, itself, may include aspects supportive of participation. The constitutions of Bolivia, Brazil, Colombia and the Philippines, for example, explicitly encourage the development and participation of NGOs at all levels of decision making (World Bank, 1997c).

In Bolivia, a new Law of Popular Participation was enacted in May 1994, setting in motion profound politico-structural changes. This law provides the legal framework for local institutions inside municipal boundaries (not recognized by the state before the passage of the law) to participate in planning, management and auditing activities related to how the law will be implemented by municipalities, how resources will be used and development activities carried out.

> *the Law of Popular Participation is seen to provide a context for users of participatory methodologies to move from micro- to macro-influencing strategies. "Empowerment" in such a context takes on a whole new meaning.* (Blackburn and de Toma, 1998)

In countries where parliaments are strong and independent, legislators can play important roles in creating a favourable environment for participation. In a critique of the World Bank's process for developing the country assistance strategy, Ghanaian NGOs noted that the strategy had:

> *...all but replaced medium and long-term national development planning... The [Bank's] consultations did not reach out to the nation's lawmakers (parliamentarians) yet, in countries where constitutional governance exists, parliaments ... have the responsibility for passing and approving legally binding commitments. Here is a legitimate question of the legality of such agreements and the implications of a lending practice that may seem, consciously or otherwise, to undermine constitutional provisions.* (ActionAid Kenya, 1998)

In the late 1980s and 1990s, many Latin American countries experienced rapid deregulation, privatization of state-owned enterprises, and the opening up of economies through imposition of structural adjustment policies. Such events increased poverty at the same time as they extended democracy. Citizens upset by steeply rising unemployment and increasing poverty became disenchanted with traditional political parties and began looking for other means of political expression. In this environment, NGOs began to focus on citizen rights and democratic accountability (Chiriboga, 1999).

Decentralization

In many countries, decentralization efforts by governments are now underway. This process is sometimes loosely equated with making government more participatory, although such a linkage is not automatic. Although decentralization seems a logical step in bringing government services closer to the people and to encouraging more local control, it can fail if steps are not taken to ensure that accountability is fostered at the local level through effective institutions and mechanisms and that government exercises fiscal restraint.

Decentralization normally means one or more of the following three things: administrative deconcentration, namely the transfer of state functions from higher to lower levels of government; fiscal decentralization or ceding of influence over budgets and financial decisions from higher to lower levels; and devolution or transfer of resources and political authority to lower-level authorities, which are mainly independent of higher levels of government. Rarely does decentralization include all three (World Bank, 1997c).

One of the principles of decentralization is to move the government closer to the people as a way of fostering greater accountability and encouraging greater local control in determining needs and problems. Local conditions, traditions and institutions are important elements in determining whether this effort is successful. For example, in Mexico, the two states of Oaxaca and Chiapas had similar endowments and development potential, and high percentages of poor and indigenous populations. Antipoverty programmes had good results in Oaxaca but poor results in Chiapas. The difference apparently was in the degree of popular participation in policy decisions and implementation. In Oaxaca, there was a long tradition of participatory mechanisms for indigenous populations and the poor. In Chiapas, however, denial of such options, coupled with widespread official corruption, led to poor services, rising tensions and armed conflict since early 1994 (World Bank, 1997c).

The important point is that decentralization will not result in greater participation and equitable distribution of benefits without careful analysis of local conditions, innovations by both central and local government, proper incentives and vibrant local institutions. In three cases analysed in Brazil, the improvements in local government that resulted in better local programmes were not brought about by decentralization but from a three-way exchange among local government, civil society and an active central government (World Bank, 1997c).

What is clear is that where state power continues to be concentrated in a centralized system, efforts to create participatory projects are often obstructed. For example, in Kenya, in the Sexually Transmitted Infections Project monitored by the Working Group, all decisions were taken by the Ministry of Health in the capital without involving either the district level medical staff or community groups. This caused delays in implementation and funding (EcoNews, Kenya, 1988).

Internal Demands for Citizen Participation

In addition to efforts undertaken by the state to devolve authority and increase involvement by citizens in their country's development, much of the current change in Southern countries is in response to demands by citizens themselves for a more active role in governance. This phenomenon has been occurring most noticeably since the fall of the Berlin Wall and the decline of communism. In some countries, this is evident in the growth of political parties. In other countries, where parties have existed for a long time and there is disenchantment with the electoral process, NGOs and other civil society groups are playing an increasingly active role in promoting citizen participation. It is clear that by their existence in countries where hitherto there were very few, NGOs and other civil society organizations are helping to create a demand for participation. As more people create or join such organizations, they are expressing their right to speak on public issues. In regions where NGOs have existed for some time, many are expanding their role beyond traditional development to participate in the advocacy arena.

The growth of such organizations over the past decade in countries, democratic or otherwise, has been dramatic (Edwards and Hulme, in Feeney, 1998):

> *NGO projects which have been put in place specifically to encourage the democratic process or to challenge undemocratic features of society and polity have been remarkably successful.* (Feeney, 1998)

Legal and Cultural Frameworks Sensitive to Participation

Regardless of the kind of government, existing traditions of the region in which a government implementing agency is operating and policies already in place can facilitate the adoption of participatory practices. The major examples of positive change described in this chapter have taken place in countries with authoritarian rule: the Philippines, Indonesia, Sri Lanka and Kenya. One such example mentioned earlier is in the Philippines where the National Irrigation Administration (NIA) transformed its operations during the autocratic rule of Ferdinand Marcos. The NIA's work was aided by several factors. There was a history of private initiative in irrigation that dated back to the early history of the country, as well as an irrigation law dating back to 1912 that recognized irrigators' associations as legal entities authorized to manage a communal irrigation system. This law also stated that farmers served by such systems would not be charged irrigation fees by the government, since the systems were not built with government funds. There also was a tradition of autonomous public entities in the countries. At the time the NIA wished to change its procedures, its charter was amended to delegate partial or full management of its national systems to irrigators' associations. Thus the legal and cultural frameworks were both conducive to instituting participatory procedures in the irrigation sector (Korten and Siy, 1988).

TRANSFORMING A GOVERNMENT IMPLEMENTING AGENCY

When government leaders have decided to change their organization and its approach, the hard work begins. An agency then needs to deal with the heart of the matter: transforming itself so fundamentally that it becomes a *facilitator* rather than a *deliverer* of development. The use of the word *transformation* communicates the dramatic nature of this change.

In Chapter 4, we assessed the extent of progress made by the World Bank and USAID in incorporating the participation of the poor and the adaptations needed in order for these complex organizations to change. This chapter makes a similar analysis of how government implementing agencies need to change. It must be recognized, however, that these agencies have a variety of constraints not present in donor organizations or even in comparable departments or ministries in Northern, industrialized countries. Some of these constraints were noted earlier in this chapter. In addition, these agencies' programmes may be forced to operate within certain political parameters determined by a ruling party, a set of elite interests, or a dominant ethnic group. They also may be required to provide the services in environments with chronic problems that make normal functioning difficult. These include poor communication, lack of infrastructure, routine power failures, lack of supplies or basic equipment and inability to attract and retain well-trained personnel due to low wages or irregular payment of wages because of inefficiencies, corruption or financial crises. Moreover, as noted at the beginning of this chapter, implementing agencies must contend with the hierarchical orientation, operating procedures, funding patterns and accountability requirements imposed by the variety of donor organizations that provide them with money.

Given the scope of change required, it is perhaps not surprising that such transformations are rare. In 1995 John Thompson noted:

> *Although calls for greater people's participation in research and development are commonly heard, it is rare to find major programmes that actively involve local people in meaningful ways, and rarer still to find such programmes being conducted by government agencies.* (Thompson, 1995)

His paper describes experiences of three government agencies – in Sri Lanka, Kenya and the Philippines – and refers to these as exceptions, though nevertheless ones that are hopeful signs that other large, technically oriented bureaucratic programmes can be reoriented to enable local people to take an active role in their own development

Organizational Elements Needing Change

Of the organizational elements needing change in large donor agencies, examples from cases monitored by the Working Group and from the literature indicate that those most important in the transformation of government implementing agencies are the following:

1 Leadership, vision and strategy
2 Organizational systems and procedures
3 Behaviour change and training
4 Internal and external change agents
5 Resources

Leadership, Vision and Strategy

At the top, leaders of government implementing agencies need to advocate new ways of doing business. They need to inspire bureaucrats to change and motivate them with a vision of the success that could result from doing things differently. In the paper mentioned above, John Thompson notes that strong leadership committed to the task of developing learning organizational systems and capacities is needed in these circumstances. The kind of change required to transform a government agency necessitates that leaders have a strong vision and enough confidence to persevere during the inevitable setbacks and challenges that will be encountered.

It is possible to incorporate participation of the poor into large-scale initiatives through dynamic leadership further down the hierarchy – at the head of a unit or team responsible for a project. In Sri Lanka, the head of the training and technical support team was a senior officer in a government development programme as well as the head of a local NGO. In that position, he was able to draw on resources from both sectors as he led a successful effort to incorporate participation of the poor into a major project (Thompson, 1995).

Organizational Systems and Procedures

In many cases of successful incorporation of the poor into government implementing agencies, pilot projects and experimentation have played significant roles. An example from Indonesia concerned efforts by the government to enable small irrigation systems to be managed by local farmer associations. The government had become concerned about the growing problem of maintenance and management of small-scale irrigation facilities in rural areas, given declining governmental resources. As a way of testing the idea of local management, the government's Irrigation Directorate and Public Works Department supported two pilot projects to involve local farmer associations in more active maintenance of the systems. Directorate and Public Works personnel had visited the Philippines National Irrigation Association – where similar efforts had been successful – prior to launching the pilot projects. These projects were successful and resulted in a new national policy to create and support farmers' associations to take over the management and maintenance of these systems (Bruns and Soelaiman, nd).

In the same Indonesian example, the Institute for Social and Economic Research, Education and Information collaborated with the Indonesian government in turning over small irrigation systems to water users. The Institute provided consultants to assist provincial irrigation service officials in instituting new procedures and took part in national working groups that drafted regulations and manuals to use in turning over the irrigation systems (Bruns and Soelaiman, nd).

Behaviour Change and Training

All the cases described in this chapter have used a learning approach to experiment with new methods and systems. In the early phases, all of them used pilot projects or experimentation that were then carefully analysed. The Kenyan project used participatory rural appraisal with very positive results. The Sri Lankan project created a hybrid approach combining participatory rural appraisal with social mobilization approaches. Each of these system changes has taken several years and requires regular monitoring and adjustments to remain effective.

Once new procedures and field practices are adopted, creative management is required for effective implementation. When the new processes and systems are applied on a larger scale, they will be tested again by the different circumstances encountered. Necessary adaptations in participatory projects can take a long time. In the case of the Philippines, fundamental changes were made to the internal management structures over more than 20 years to help the agency carry out its new participatory strategy. No fewer than seven major innovations were undertaken (Thompson, 1995).

The institutional changes described in this chapter required development of trust between and among government personnel, secondary stakeholders and the poor, along with changes in behaviour, in order to create and operate new systems and procedures. The various interests and perceptions of the different parties needed to be accommodated. Where such trust and new behaviour are absent, it is unlikely that positive change will occur. In one of the World Bank-funded cases monitored by the Working Group, the Community-managed Schools Programme in El Salvador, such was the case. The principal aim of the project was to reintroduce primary education up to the sixth year to rural zones of extreme poverty that had not been served by the national education system. The administrators and teachers, however, were very resistant to delegation and inclusion of parents to take part in the administrative processes of the school, which was a major emphasis of the project. Parents' involvement was blocked by the administrative system itself. Thus, the hoped for participation of the poor was not realized (Tandon and Cordeiro, 1990). In another case reviewed from Zimbabwe, the importance of personality types was noted as a key element in whether attitudes could be changed.

> *It is doubtful whether staff who have been professionally socialized and to a certain extent conditioned under colonial rule can truly reverse top-down approaches as this would force them to question most of their working*

> *life. The same applies to older farmers who have accepted a subordinate role and now identify with it. The impact chiefly depends, therefore, on the personality of each individual agricultural extension worker. One cannot expect this to be uniform.* (Hagmann, Chuma and Murwira, 1998)

The learning approach, which is a common denominator in the various examples cited here, is an important departure from the traditional procedures used by large donor organizations. These include the World Bank's project cycle, goal-oriented planning used by GTZ, and DFID's logical framework. All three of these methods have built-in rigidities and time frames that work against the trial-and-error approach necessary when using participatory processes.

In describing the NIA experience in the Philippines, Frances Korten outlined a participatory process to institute changes that involved five interrelated learning stages:

1   Identify and evaluate aspects of the institution's programmes and practices that are not meeting its objectives – or the people's needs – and require significant improvement, modification or rejection.
2   Develop a new, more dynamic, participatory approach and test it on a small scale under different ecological and socioeconomic conditions.
3   Draw lessons of relevance to applying the approach on a broader scale following a period of experimentation, assessment and adjustment.
4   Analyse and integrate lessons into forms and procedures that can be applied widely throughout all levels of the institution.
5   Develop capacities throughout the organization and incorporate the appropriate changes into the agency's routines.

She noted that the identification of a need for institutional reorientation and innovation gradually leads to improved practices on an agency-wide level. Regular discussion, analysis and adjustment are required to keep the process on track (Korten and Siy, 1988).

Obviously, training is essential to any organizational change and must be seen as a long-term effort intended to change attitudes, build confidence, provide new skills and encourage regular experimentation and analysis. It also must be incorporated into a wider programme of human resource development that includes other personnel issues, such as recruitment of new staff with needed expertise, and development of new incentives and rewards for successful participatory work.

Internal and External Change Agents

In the same way that large donor organizations created alliances with NGO activists to promote policy change, the same is true for government implementing agencies intent on integrating participation of the poor into their operations. In the cases examined in this chapter, small teams of innovative and committed agency professionals worked in collaboration with others. In Kenya, SIDA and the International Institute for Environment and Development provided assistance. In the Philippines, the Communal Working Group (also called the Communal Irrigation Committee) had both NIA staff and outside social scientists, management specialists and agricultural engineers. In Sri Lanka, the Regional Development Division of the Ministry of Policy Planning and Implementation, when looking for ways to create an institutional training capacity in participatory planning at the national level, created alliances with local NGOs, universities and other groups with participatory expertise. In Indonesia, the Institute for Social and Economic Research, Education and Information joined forces with the Ministry of Public Works to develop ways of turning over small irrigation systems to water users' associations.

Resources

In donor organizations, the availability of money to support change efforts may be the most important issue related to resources. In regard to implementing agencies, however, how and when resources are made available to change efforts, and the conditions under which these resources are given, may be the most important issues. In most recipient government programmes, once the initiative is agreed upon, large sums of donor money are disbursed and quick measurable results are hoped for. However, time frames are often unrealistic in terms of how long it takes for participatory processes to yield results. What is needed to foster participation is a gradual disbursement of funds, with small amounts being made available early on during the formulation phases of projects when trust is being established, and donor and implementing government agency personnel are establishing relationships with primary stakeholders, negotiating terms, and agreeing on pilot projects or other experimental processes. In at least three cases reviewed, donors provided long-term financing and flexible arrangements to support the changes underway. In Sri Lanka, the two donors, the International Fund for Agricultural Development (IFAD) and the UNDP, agreed to a seven-year time frame within which to develop the new approach, and disbursed funds more slowly than more conventional investment projects (Thompson, 1995). In Kenya, SIDA provided long-term funding and limited intervention in

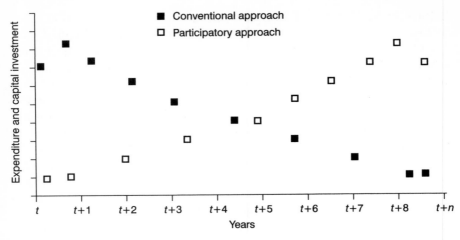

Source: Thompson, 1995

Figure 5.1 *Conventional financing contrasted with participatory financing*

internal affairs of the Soil and Water Conservation Branch, thereby allowing experimentation and necessary adjustments (Thompson, 1995). In the Philippines, the Ford Foundation provided flexible grants to the NIA and assisting institutions, such as the communal irrigation committee, a working group that guided the transformation process (Thompson, 1995).

Figure 5.1 contrasts the differences between the conventional approach to project financing and the participatory approach. The conventional approach begins with a large infusion of money and declines gradually over seven to eight years, whereas the participatory approach begins with a very small amount of money and gradually increases until Year 8, when it begins to decline.

Monitoring and Evaluation

Monitoring and evaluation are often neglected when carrying out development projects. Although they are important to all initiatives, they are essential in times of dramatic change in order to check progress, make corrections and track results. Such monitoring is particularly important when a government implementing agency is making efforts to incorporate primary stakeholder participation into its operations. An example is the case of the PROINDER project in Argentina, funded by the World Bank and monitored by the local housing and social service organization (SEHAS).

The project, itself, had developed a 'participatory monitoring plan', which enabled participation of NGOs and primary stakeholders in monitoring the development of the project. The focus was on participatory preparation and monitoring of subprojects and participation in decision making within provincial units and the National Coordination Commission. SEHAS noted that the monitoring and evaluation processes did not enable evaluation of capacity building and empowerment of primary stakeholders. In addition, various participants, including a small sample of primary stakeholders were interviewed regarding their involvement in the project. They were asked about their knowledge of the project, their level of participation in it, their expectations, how they felt their participation was valued and their suggestions to improve it. These findings were shared with government officials at the national level and World Bank officials.

SEHAS also strengthened a small NGO coalition to be a consulting mechanism for the project. Subsequently, the monitoring team was asked by both the government and the World Bank to contribute ideas regarding monitoring indicators of primary stakeholder involvement in the project and the level of empowerment achieved. The Argentine Rural Development Department found the independent monitoring process so valuable that they wrote to SEHAS thanking them for their involvement and ideas (Baima de Borri et al, 1998).

In the Kenya case funded by SIDA, after using a participatory approach for five years but before full participation had been achieved, impact studies showed significant results such as improved productivity, decreased land degradation and an increased capacity of local groups to manage their own productive resources from the new methods. Moreover, the studies also showed that participation had created closer ties and more understanding between farmers and Ministry staff (Thompson, 1995).

In addition to monitoring and evaluation, Thompson noted that regular documentation and analysis of lessons learned in a project were essential in order to improve practice and build an institutional memory. In the Philippines, three documentation efforts were a part of the training programme used to help staff adapt to the new methodology. The first documented the relationships of the principal activities of the technical staff, the farmers and the community organizers in the form of process reports and was made available to all. The second was detailed case studies on management issues encountered in the participatory projects, later used in training courses for other NIA staff. The third method was to combine site visits by the working group members with workshops for the project coordinators where emerging problems and issues were examined (Thompson, 1995).

WHAT DONORS CAN DO

Although change in government implementing agencies is primarily the work of those agencies, there is much that donors can do to aid these efforts.

Global Changes in the Development Paradigm

In recent years, an important shift in donor/client relationships has been launched through the Organisation for Economic Cooperation and Development/Development Assistance Committee (OECD/DAC) – the forum which reflects advances in thinking and practice of bilateral donor agencies. In its *21st Century Partnership Statement*, adopted in May 1996, the DAC committed itself to a set of common development goals to be reached by the year 2015 (OECD/DAC, 1996). These goals cover economic well-being, social development and environmental sustainability. In the document, the donors also committed themselves to work in a more coordinated way at the national level and to have consistent policies that are supportive of development (referred to as policy coherence – donor policies in one area will not undermine those in another). These changes were instituted in order to align themselves more with national development strategies formulated by recipient countries themselves.

Certain obstacles stand in the way, however. One obvious problem is that representatives of developing country governments were not participants in any of the discussions, negotiations or agreements reached to create this commitment. Yet they are expected to participate 'on the frontlines' in reaching these goals in their own countries. Another is the fact that bilateral donors are dependent on their legislatures for the money they use in overseas aid. This means that the political desires and self-interests of legislators and voters in the Northern countries will be incorporated into their programmes. This inhibits donors from being as responsive to recipient governments' needs and priorities as they may wish to be.

Since this new vision for a global partnership was agreed upon in 1996, there has been a perceived lack of effort by the donors to adjust their aid programmes to work towards these goals. Only if donors and recipient governments set interim targets and work together towards these goals can they be realized. By early 1998, 21 indicators of progress had been developed by the DAC in order to set baselines and milestones to show progress made towards the goals. Thus far, this effort seems more rhetorical than actual. In spite of its obstacles, however, the statement represents an important first step towards creating partnerships with developing country governments.

Introduced in late 1998 at the World Bank, the Comprehensive Development Framework represents a more inclusive approach to development at the national level than previously embraced by the World Bank or other donors. The intention is to have national governments in 'the driver's seat' as regards development plans, goals and strategies to carry them out. Multilateral and bilateral donors, and a country's civil society and business community would all be involved with the government in determining a clear vision for national development and in setting goals towards sustainable growth and poverty alleviation. The approach focuses attention on all important aspects of a country's development including governance, law, finance, education, health, other social issues, technology and infrastructure.

This initiative was founded in 1999 and will continue to be adapted over a ten-year period.

Effective Use of Aid

In 1998, the World Bank published a study on aid effectiveness as part of a larger 'rethinking of aid' being undertaken by the international community. Such reflection has been brought on by the end of the Cold War and the growth of integrated capital markets. Another impetus, according to the report, is the rethinking of the role of assistance by both developing and developed nations in the light of a new paradigm that holds that 'effective aid supports institutional development and policy reforms that are at the heart of successful development' (Dollar and Pritchett, 1998).

The report has two key themes. These are that effective aid requires the right timing and the right mix of money and ideas. Well-timed financial assistance to countries which are actually reforming their policies can increase the benefits of reform and maintain popular support for them. At the local level, aid can make a positive difference if provided when communities are organizing themselves to improve service. The key is that countries must be working to improve their policies and institutions in order for financial assistance to have a major impact.

The report highlights several salient points in regard to the participation of the poor and the reform of government implementing agencies. Active involvement of civil society in countries under reform can help sustain sound management and improve public services. In cases where aid projects have used a participatory approach to service delivery, huge improvements have often resulted. The report notes that a top-down, technocratic approach to project design and service delivery has failed in areas critical for development, such as rural water supply, primary education and natural resource management.

In relation to the main finding that aid works best in countries under reform, it says that in countries that have not undertaken reform, 'ideas will be more useful than large-scale finance' (Dollar and Pritchett, 1998). Here the report notes that the traditional 'approval and disbursement culture' of large donors has meant that small-scale, staff-intensive efforts to improve institutions and service delivery have not been valued or supported. This is a particularly important point given the report's finding that the most critical contribution aid projects make is not to increase funding to a particular sector but rather to improve service delivery through strengthening sectoral and local institutions (Dollar and Pritchett, 1998).

Creating the Will to Practice Participation

Although many donor agencies now promote participation, relatively few recipient governments actively incorporate such practices into their work. As the Working Group report on monitoring World Bank projects shows, for many governments, there is still a lack of clarity as to what participation entails, and no appreciation for what gains can be made towards more effective projects as a result of participation. Many governments still think of primary stakeholders as passive recipients of project benefits, not as active stakeholders (Tandon and Cordeiro, 1998).

What can be done to create the will needed in governments to incorporate participation into their work, and to make the institutional adjustments which such a change will necessitate? Global efforts have been described in the previous sections. In addition, across the spectrum of multilateral and bilateral donor agencies, many mid-level staff are making efforts to persuade recipient government agencies to use participatory methods. However, to take one example, attitudes of some World Bank staff reveal the continuing uncertainty about the organization's responsibility to ensure participation. In 1998 InterAction, the US NGO consortium, conducted an assessment of participation by the poor in the identification phase of 19 World Bank projects.

> *Task team leaders interviewed reported that they were not confident enough about the Bank's commitment to quality participation to clearly define their approach [to participation in a specific project] in terms of staff, funds and other resources before the loan is approved.* (InterAction, 1999)

Senior staff and heads of donor agencies also need to be directly involved in promoting participation. Delegates at the 1998

Participation Conference described participatory projects as only 'islands of excellence' unless the environment in which they take place becomes more open and supportive of this approach at all levels. Their recommendations called for policy dialogue between donors and recipient governments on the need for, and value of, participation. Second, they called for 'partnerships for participation', involving donors, NGOs and governments where forums would be held for interaction and negotiation on the topic of participation, to determine how they can work together to make it happen (Group Three-A, 1998).

Beginning such change can be enormously challenging in countries where relationships and informal systems are entrenched. Donor agencies, however, can play an important role in the way in which they go about working with such governments in specific projects. In describing the World Bank project in Pakistan, which was the topic of the case study mentioned earlier in this chapter, Van Wicklin says:

> *the Bank staff concluded that the 'highly politicized relations based on criteria of family, tribe, ethnicity' in government had to be transformed in order for participation to work. The project focus was on creating a more open, participatory culture within government as a prerequisite to widespread popular participation. The Pakistan project focused on reorienting the government towards demand-led policy dialogue and reform prior to making substantial infrastructure investments. Although it faced significant political resistance at first, persistence paid off with the development of a more accountable, professional civil service that included community representatives on policy committees for the first time.* (Van Wicklin, 1998)

The World Bank still feels handicapped in promoting participation to recipient governments.

> *While the Bank is having some success in convincing governments to be more responsive to and accepting of participation, its track record depends on the degree to which governments are interested, supportive, and willing to invest in participation... Projects ... ultimately belong to governments to prepare and implement. This relationship constitutes both the Bank's comparative advantage and the single largest constraint to mainstreaming participation in its operations.* (Aycrigg, 1998)

Although it is true that World Bank-funded projects do belong to the government, there is more the organization can do to encourage government implementing agencies to incorporate participation. If the World Bank follows its own recommendations from its report on aid effectiveness, it can work to convince recipient governments to undertake participation on the basis that it is an effective development strategy. Together with this, the World Bank – and other donors – could create incentives for recipient governments to prepare projects and policies in a participatory way.

CONCLUSION

As this chapter shows, there are still relatively few examples of government implementing agencies that have transformed development programmes. With more organizational changes underway in the past few years and more efforts being made by donor agencies to promote these changes, a momentum in favour of participation is growing. Promising signs can be seen in the examples analysed in this chapter and from policy changes being made by donors. However, there is still a very long way to go!

Four lessons can be drawn from the review of these cases.

Lesson One

Donors can have significant influence on recipient government implementing agencies in favour of participation by the poor.
Although it is clear that donor organizations cannot force recipient governments to embark on a path of change, there are many things they can do to help create the frameworks and incentives necessary, and actually to aid in the change process itself with a government implementing agency.

Lesson Two

Principles and approaches needed to transform government implementing agencies have been tested and proven successful.
Although there are not many cases of implementing agencies or large development projects that have incorporated participation of the poor into their practices, those that have been reviewed in this chapter show that there are common principles and approaches that have been used successfully in different countries and contexts. The need for imaginative leadership, a learning approach to project development, regular monitoring and evaluation, and flexible, long-term

funding and adaptations in systems and procedures are elements that have been applied successfully in a variety of settings. Therefore, potential change agents in government implementing agencies have guidelines from other projects elsewhere to help them as they institute a process of transformation.

Lesson Three

NGOs and other local participants can and must play key roles if change is to be successful on a large scale.
Experiences analysed in this chapter show the importance of involving NGOs in changes in large-scale development projects. If government agencies, together with large donors, are to break out of their traditional bureaucratic project designs, they must seek input from NGOs, researchers, and local organizations that have important relevant experience with grassroots populations. Involving participants who understand how to work with the poor and facilitate change in local communities is essential to government agencies as they adopt a learning approach to project design.

> *Linked organizations are critical: no single body can go it alone successfully. Creating and managing useful links, building up a coalition of support are key management tasks. In environmental work links may be as much with environmental movements and key individuals as with formal groups.* (Shepherd, 1998)

Lesson Four

Donors cannot expect changes in government agencies until they, themselves, incorporate participation of the poor.
Donors must first do the hard work of turning their own rhetoric into reality through systematic changes in their own organizations. At the same time, they can continue to use their leverage to help create favourable environments and incentives for countries to change. Some progress has been made in information disclosure, fostering accountability, greater transparency and participation in policy formulation processes in developing countries, and in designing impressive participatory projects, although they remain isolated as 'islands of excellence'.

Much more remains to be done to reorient the practices of both donor institutions and recipient governments so that participation of the poor becomes the order of the day in development. Donors, recipient government agencies and civil society organizations need to work together in a more productive way. No one entity has the ability to change these patterns and habits alone. We all need each other to do things right.

Chapter 6

Lessons Learned and Implications for Participation of the Poor

INTRODUCTION

Having completed this analysis, what is our overall assessment of progress in incorporating participation of the poor into donor organizations and government implementing agencies? Have the donors adequately adopted participatory practices in their work? To what extent have they made the organizational reforms necessary to incorporate participation into their organizations? What is needed to assist government implementing agencies to take on this task in a serious way? Lastly, how can we assess the roles NGOs have played in integrating primary stakeholder participation into donor organizations? What meaning can be derived from the fact that NGOs and donors have had such an intense and enduring engagement on this topic?

LESSONS LEARNED

Participation in Development Initiatives

This review of donor experiences has shown that, although participation of primary stakeholders in the preparation and implementation phases of projects is recognized as essential, actual participation in the earliest phase of project formulation, later in monitoring during implementation, and, finally, in evaluation is very small. Moreover, the quality of such participation is not always what it should be. Participation of the poor in policy formulation holds substantial promise for changing the fundamental way such policies are developed.

BOX 6.1 LESSONS FOR PARTICIPATION IN PROJECTS AND FORMULATION OF DEVELOPMENT POLICY

1   Disseminate all information needed to make primary stakeholder participation both realistic and useful.
2   Use trial and error and feedback and be flexible in project development or policy formulation to make necessary adjustments as information becomes known or conditions change.
3   Improve the skills of all stakeholders to engage in participatory project and policy development.
4   Increase the quantity and improve the quality of participation by the poor.

Rajesh Tandon has called for five steps to be taken to advance the participation of the poor. The first is that donor agencies ought to institute independent internal reviews to monitor progress. This could be done through a review of a random sample of projects, joint reviews with independent people outside the donor agency, or perhaps by establishing a participation ombudsman. A second necessary step, embedded in the first lesson above, is to establish or expand transparency and accountability mechanisms in donor agencies. Paramount in this effort would be the establishment of *minimum quality standards* for participatory elements such as information dissemination, capacity building and policy development. The third point is that participatory monitoring and evaluation should be strengthened, and made a systematic part of project or policy development and implementation. Included in this should be accountability to both the donor as well as to all stakeholders. The fourth step is to continue to promote participation of the poor in policy formulation in order to root policy formulation within the country's own requirements and to forge the consensus necessary for later implementation. The fifth recommendation is to operate within a framework of continuous learning and action (Tandon, 1998b). Given the complexities encountered in particular project contexts, such an approach is essential. Although there are excellent tools that have been developed for use in participation (participatory rural appraisal being the foremost among them), they cannot be used routinely. Those who carry out participation initiatives must always be students of their processes as well as facilitators.

Formidable difficulties remain in integrating participatory methodology throughout donor programmes. World Bank structural adjustment programmes in 1999 constituted 63 per cent of all lending done through the International Bank for Reconstruction and

Development (BIC, 1999).[1] Adjustment loans are developed very quickly and involve no participation whatsoever. Most of the effort in participation has been with socially oriented projects such as in health, education, agriculture and natural resource management. Adjustment loans represent huge sums of money.

> *Current practice of [information] disclosure on adjust-ment lending precludes the affected public from any input into the decision-making process, although in many countries the public is now being asked to play a monitor-ing role and is supposed to have input into the lending process through the Poverty Reduction Strategy Paper and the Comprehensive Development Framework (CDF).* (BIC, 1999)

Adjustment lending has been impervious to participation. Whether the Poverty Reduction Strategy Paper can begin to change that reality remains to be seen. Like adjustment loans, large infrastructure projects normally have not been the focus of participatory methods either at the World Bank or in other donor agencies. Bilateral donors also have constraints placed on certain politically important develop-ment initiatives by the country's executive branch of government, its congress or parliament. Incorporating participation of the poor into such projects remains a major challenge or may even be precluded.

Nevertheless, even if donors succeed only in completing the job of integrating participation of the poor into socially oriented projects, that would represent a major breakthrough for development. Successful donors would then have more dynamic programmes in which the energy, creativity and support of all stakeholders would be channelled towards sustainable change. This presents quite a differ-ent picture than today in many donor-funded projects!

Incorporating Participation of the Poor into International Development Agencies

At the heart of the effort to incorporate participation of the poor into development is the need for donor organizational reform. This book has examined in detail the efforts undertaken by two donors: the World Bank and USAID. Lessons learned from their experiences can be applied in some measure to GTZ and the early efforts by DFID.

In the Working Group monitoring report on Bank initiatives, it is noted that the very design and structure of international donor organi-zations and government implementing agencies are central to moving participation forward (Tandon and Cordeiro, 1998). Tandon

---

BOX 6.2 LESSONS FOR INCORPORATING PARTICIPATION OF THE POOR IN INTERNATIONAL DEVELOPMENT AGENCIES

1   Leaders must promote and act on a clear vision of change.
2   Staff must be given the opportunity to influence, understand and accept changes that affect them.
3   Fundamental change will be achieved only if structures and systems are altered appropriately.
4   Systematically monitoring progress of major change is essential to achieve ultimate success.
5   Boards of directors must be aligned with the new vision, and the institutional changes needed to realize it.

---

reinforced this point in his synthesis presentation at the conference when he said that organizational renewal and reform are now the most important steps to take if incorporation of participation by the poor is to be successful. As a way to promote this in all the donor agencies, NGOs called for the strengthening of a nascent participation network which had been started among donors, NGOs and the IDS through their joint planning of the conference itself. Such a network should expand to involve recipient governments, NGOs, academics and others (Tandon, 1998b). This had been the original vision for the IGP.

What exactly is the nature of the changes that these donor agencies have undertaken? Fox and Brown note that the literature on organizational change distinguishes between organizational *adaptation* and organizational *learning* in large bureaucracies.

> *Organizational adaptation involves changes in behavior in response to new pressures or incentives, but without any adjustments in the organization's underlying goals, priorities, or decision-making processes. Learning, in contrast, involves disseminating new conceptual frameworks and institutional changes throughout an organization, thus leading to qualitatively new goals and priorities, as well as changes in behavior.* (Fox and Brown, 1998)

Although these are not mutually exclusive ideas, the record shows that:

> *adaptive behavior is common, whereas true learning is rare. The very nature of institutions is such that the dice are loaded in favor of the less demanding behavior associated with adaptation.* (Haas, 1990)

Fox and Brown note that most observers tend to conclude that the World Bank adapts more than it learns, and thus does not change fundamentally. This seems to be the case as well in the other donor agencies reviewed, based on their participatory efforts.

Can the momentum for change propel these agencies forward to embrace the reforms necessary to incorporate participation? Although the desire to retain control and the tendency to continue to design programmes in the traditional way remain strong in donor organizations, the reforms and innovations may be signs of a fundamental change in donors – and in development as a whole. As noted earlier in this book, observers think that many World Bank staff have had an attitude change, and now understand that their expert knowledge is not enough to ensure well-designed programmes and sustainable results. Robert Chambers from the IDS has written extensively about how hard it is for development professionals in donor agencies to change their view of the poor. These are highly educated people who have been successful in a hierarchical, intellectually oriented environment. To be able to understand, accept and pursue a participatory methodology that requires valuing the knowledge expressed by poor people – often uneducated and sometimes illiterate – requires a fundamental philosophical change (Chambers, 1997).

An example from Zimbabwe illustrates the difficulty of such a change even where the gap is much smaller:

> ...*a change in the attitudes of extension staff towards smallholder farmers is the key determinant for the success of the approach. In a hierarchically structured society, where hierarchy is based mostly on the level of formal education, it is difficult for formally educated staff to accept farmers' traditional- and experience-based knowledge systems as equal, and to learn from them.* (Hagmann et al, 1998)

In addition to attitude change, the World Bank and other donors that are inclined to adopt participation of the poor can be encouraged by recent research findings that may help change development thinking in general. The recent study *Assessing Aid*, which analyses the most successful ways in which to provide aid, notes that properly channelled aid can help improve institutions and policies at the sector level. Of central importance in this is the participation of the poor. The report notes that 'beneficiary participation can quintuple project success' (Dollar and Pritchett, 1998). In a review of donor-financed rural water supply projects, those with high beneficiary participation

---

BOX 6.3 LESSONS FOR INCORPORATING PARTICIPATION OF THE POOR IN GOVERNMENT IMPLEMENTING AGENCIES

1   Donors can have significant influence on recipient government implementing agencies in favour of participation of the poor.
2   Principles and approaches needed to transform government implementing agencies have been tested and proven successful.
3   NGOs and other local participants can and must play key roles if change is to be successful on a large scale.
4   Donors cannot expect changes in government implementing agencies until they, themselves, incorporate participation of the poor.

---

had a 68 per cent success rate as opposed to those with low participation, which had only a 12 per cent rate (Narayan et al, 1995). The report goes on to say that participatory provision of services ultimately requires that citizens have a voice, and thus promotes greater freedom of expression by citizens – one of the keys to creating a more democratic environment (Narayan et al, 1998).

The reasons preventing these bureaucracies from making the changes needed for incorporating participation of the poor are formidable – governance structures, entrenched systems and procedures, competing demands, resources and anti-reform forces. The central question remains whether bureaucracies as large and political as those reviewed in this book can become learning organizations with the flexibility necessary for participatory development. Is it possible? Only time will tell.

Incorporating Participation of the Poor in Government Implementing Agencies

Incorporating participation of the poor into government implementing agencies represents the frontier in this work. Although relatively little has been achieved, there is reason for optimism and the lessons learned are encouraging.

Although there are few written examples of participation in public agencies, those that are available hold promise in several respects. Donors such as the World Bank have insisted for years that projects are the responsibility of the recipient government, and, therefore, the World Bank cannot impose participation on them. However, in cases reviewed in this book in which donors (including the World Bank) have made efforts to influence implementing agencies, they have often been successful. These cases also show that the willingness of donors to alter their normal funding patterns, design procedures and systems to assist participatory efforts is essential to success.

Donor representatives interested in promoting participation in implementing agencies need also to look for the true agents of change in these organizations. They may be surprised to discover who these agents are. Thompson describes a participatory social assessment in an agricultural programme in Estonia, funded by the World Bank:

> *the Bank had assumed that social scientists from Estonia Agricultural University would be the appropriate actors to be conducting the participatory social assessments and supporting the establishment of local land and water associations. [This proved problematic, however, as] the scientists were resistant to handing over control of these participatory analyses to the farmers. Instead, the Ministry of Agriculture engineers were more adept at learning from farmers and setting the participatory tone for the fieldwork.* (Thompson, 1998)

At the Participation Conference, Rajesh Tandon urged building country-level partnerships and capacity for incorporating participation of the poor. The distinctive feature in such a partnership would be that it would be society-led and not government-led – donor-led. Such a partnership would include an explicit national participation strategy and a systematic public information disclosure process. These efforts would be independently monitored and lessons learned would be shared with other countries (Tandon, 1998b).

MAJOR LESSONS LEARNED

Lesson One

Incorporating participation of the poor into a large donor agency or a government implementing agency is a long-term process.
What is striking in this analysis is that one or even two decades may be necessary in order to institute and fully carry out an organizational transformation to incorporate a new methodology such as participation of the poor. GTZ began its focus on the poor in 1986, and, by its own account, the change is far from complete. The World Bank began studying participation in 1990, and its management readily admit that the task is only partly accomplished. USAID started its reform process in 1993 and continues to make corrections and to implement changes seven years later. As a recent USAID paper said:

> *The next two to three years will be critical to consolidate changes and achieve tangible and lasting performance improvements. If we slow down at this stage, we will be left with an incompatible mix of old and new structures, guidance, and processes, and the desired performance improvements will not materialize.* (USAID, 1999)

In similar fashion, the government implementing agencies reviewed here that undertook to incorporate participation of the poor have all needed a decade or more to carry out changes. The best known of these, the NIA in the Philippines, took 20 years to complete its changes, and had no fewer than seven major innovations. In one of the more recent changes in the agricultural extension service in one province in Zimbabwe, it was said that:

> *Despite the favourable conditions that exist in Masvingo province, the effective institutionalization of participatory innovation development and extension in the agricultural extension service will require a process of at least 5 to 10 years. Continuous commitment by the institution as well as by donors during this period is considered critical to its success.* (Hagmann et al, 1998)

Implications of this for donors, government implementing agencies and others such as NGOs are significant in terms of funding, staffing, willingness to engage over a long period of time and to monitor efforts regularly and adapt as needed, with the expectation that results may not be apparent for some time. In a certain sense, using a participatory methodology means that change will be ongoing, and that adaptations and flexibility to shifting circumstances will be necessary for the foreseeable future. If a donor organization has embraced a learning approach, it may succeed in incorporating the participation methodology, but it will probably never stop adapting and changing as conditions require.

Lesson Two

Primary ingredients for successful organizational change are commitment of the leadership, a strategic approach, a learning environment and participation throughout the organization.
Chapter 4 compared the incremental change approach at the World Bank with the transformational approach at USAID. As noted, USAID made a strategic decision at the top to adopt reform. Many, although not all, of its senior managers were behind it and the agency began

altering all its systems and practices to incorporate it. The threat to USAID's survival from the US Congress interfered, however, distracting attention from the reforms. Moreover, insufficient opportunity to understand, influence and accept the changes was provided in the early years. Moving from a hierarchical orientation to a participatory, team-based approach was fraught with unforeseen problems. To its credit, USAID has monitored the reforms, reinstituted training, sought regular input from its partners regarding their concerns and continued to make corrections to ensure proper implementation of the changes.

The World Bank had used a learning approach in the early years, which enabled experimentation and gave staff time to examine, debate and understand the topic of participation and its potential value to the organization. After an informal participation policy was adopted in 1994, experimentation and learning continued, facilitated by resources from the FIAHS and later from the Strategic Compact. However, the World Bank has yet to develop an organizational strategy to incorporate participation, has never adopted a formal participation policy, has not garnered widespread support from senior management for this issue, nor has it adjusted the project cycle or tried to change the 'move the money' mentality.

One would have to say that at this point USAID has a better chance of succeeding with its organizational reform towards participation than the World Bank does. USAID has more of the necessary ingredients: commitment of its leadership and many senior managers; a strategic orientation; and a learning approach based on monitoring efforts and continued consultation with its partners on reform implementation. If the new administrator who took charge in 2001 continues the commitment to change, reforms should go forward.

Prospects at the World Bank are less clear. Without an organizational strategy, a formal policy or commitment from senior managers below the president, and with tighter budgets since the end of the Strategic Compact, incorporating participation is at risk. A learning environment continues among some of its staff and may spread, given the adoption of required participatory processes such as the poverty reduction strategy. Participation proponents in the World Bank need more organizational support to move forward, however.

Lesson Three

An 'inside-outside' strategy is essential to major organizational change, both in terms of policy and practice.
The Chapter 2 case study clearly shows that the interaction of NGOs and the World Bank was an essential ingredient in results achieved in the participation of the poor. The early advocacy work by environ-

mental NGOs created the political context into which participation was introduced. NGO support for the Learning Group in the early days was important for its survival and continued engagement over a decade served to keep participation alive at the World Bank. NGOs and World Bank staff formed informal alliances at different levels inside the organization, each side providing moral support and practical assistance to the other: the insiders struggled to make Bank initiatives participatory in spite of agency impediments; the outsiders searched for leverage points to promote and advance the topic. NGO interest also served to ensure accountability.

The impact at the World Bank might have been more significant if development and environmental NGOs had created formal alliances and worked together more strategically towards common goals. As it was, they tended to work separately, sharing information from time to time and occasionally coming together for a joint World Bank meeting or short-term effort.

The record of engagement between the Working Group and the World Bank over the past decade shows the advantages to both sides of critical cooperation (see Chapter 2). The NGOs have been able to promote the participation of the poor on a wide scale through the work of the World Bank. For their part, the donors have gained from this relationship with NGOs and have benefited from the constant attention to their monitoring of participation and by joint strategies for pushing reforms. This engagement has also served from time to time to improve the image of the World Bank. The Working Group has always needed to remain clear and consistent about its own advocacy objectives, and remain alert so as to avoid efforts at co-option by the World Bank.

An inside/outside strategy is also essential to the practice of participation by the poor by both donor organizations and government implementing agencies. NGOs, local organizations, academics, foundations and specialized institutes need to be included in order for donor and recipient government agencies to benefit from their experience and support.

In terms of the reform of implementing agencies, what has also been striking is that when these agencies have committed themselves to change, they have readily welcomed outsiders to work with them. In virtually all of the cases reviewed in this book, the particular ministry, government service or project worked hand-in-hand with outsiders from donor agencies, NGOs, foundations, local universities and other local organizations.

Lesson Four

Advocacy campaigns of long duration need to be able to create and maintain momentum, learn from experience and create coalitions for maximum impact.

NGOs began promoting participation of the poor in World Bank initiatives as long ago as 1987 and environmental NGOs began advocating for full information disclosure four years before that. These two campaigns have continued since then, mostly on parallel tracks and on occasions jointly.

For the Working Group to advocate effectively, several challenges must be taken into account. Its members are individual organizations or networks across the world and which World Bank reform is one of many issues on their agenda. Within the area of World Bank reform itself, a variety of issues are taken up by the Working Group, with only one or two people charged with coordination of a topic at the global level. Resources and time, communication challenges and the ability to agree on and coordinate strategy are among the major challenges. Although the Working Group has a secretariat function, it is a small, low-cost effort in a Southern country far from World Bank headquarters and other members. This contrasts with other advocacy campaigns, some of which rely on a strong, constant presence in Washington, DC, and where activists work full-time on World Bank reform. In these cases, they can inform and assist campaign activists in other parts of the world and can relate daily with the World Bank.

In the case of the Working Group's work on participation, there have been several high and low points of effectiveness during its many years of work. Prior to the creation of the Learning Group, NGOs in the Working Group promoted popular participation only when the NGO–World Bank Committee met. The Working Group supported the creation of the Learning Group, made recommendations and monitored its progress but without benefit of a clear strategy. The March 1991 NGO–World Bank Steering Committee meeting at which the *Saly Declaration* was written was a promising moment, but NGO members did not immediately create a strategy to implement it. It was only in 1994 that the Working Group reinvigorated the subgroup on participation and created a strategy that they carried out, culminating in the November 1998 Participation Conference. This was possible because of participation expertise present in the subgroup, leadership, a strategic orientation, and commitment of time and resources by several NGO members of the steering committee and the committee at large. By this time, Working Group membership was primarily that of Southern NGOs.

For the first decade of advocacy on participation, there was almost no effort by development and environmental NGOs to collaborate across campaigns. In fact, as noted in Chapter 2, their strategies in 1992 clashed head on in the IDA–10 replenishment process. Several years later, beginning in 1997 and continuing to the present day, environmental and development NGOs have made intermittent efforts to collaborate – it will be important to collaborate more systematically in the future.

The Working Group's strategic decisions in three areas were the key to the results they achieved. These were the decentralization of the group, beginning in 1995; undertaking monitoring of World Bank-funded projects and policy formulation processes in early 1997; and mobilizing the World Bank and other donors to sponsor the 1998 Participation Conference.

The decentralization of the Working Group is now well underway and is altering the nature of its advocacy on World Bank reform. How the various regional assemblies work together on issues of global concern is still being considered. The participation of the poor campaign is not over. How well it succeeds in the future will depend on how well the expanded Working Group is able to craft its continuing strategy, create coalitions and find key leverage points at country, regional and headquarters levels.

Lesson Five

Donors, civil society, government and parliamentarians need to work together to promote participation of the poor in recipient countries. It is certainly true that donors cannot force government implementing agencies to incorporate participation of the poor in their programmes. But it is also true that donors can do far more than they have thus far to motivate, influence, train and assist such agencies to do so. The OECD/DAC partnership framework and the World Bank's comprehensive development framework are new positive examples of what can be done. In projects themselves, changes in donor policies and practices that SIDA has undertaken – more flexible funding arrangements, a learning approach to project design and adaptations in donor procedures – have led to changes in approach by recipient government personnel responsible for projects and impressive results in the projects themselves.

What is also encouraging is that, although relatively few implementing agencies or large development projects have incorporated the participation of the poor, those that have succeeded all used very similar principles and methods. These have included imaginative leadership, an iterative process of project design, regular participatory monitoring, flexible, long-term funding, and adaptations in systems and procedures. Successful consultations in policy formulation processes have also revealed a straightforward set of 'do's and don'ts' for effective engagement with civil society organizations, assuming the political will to do so is present.

As noted in Chapter 5, where NGOs and others are involved with recipient governments and donors, successful change is more likely in projects and policy formulation. This inclusive approach must become the norm if development is to succeed on a large scale. As Rajesh Tandon has noted:

> *Much of the discussion of participation has happened between Bank and other bilateral agencies and NGOs or with official government agency bureaucrats, but we need to bring in parliamentarians. We need to bring in trade unions and cooperatives. We need to bring in people from media and academia, people from the faith and culture and art and music because they all constitute important segments of our society and without having systematic dialogue with them, it will not be possible to generate the kind of country level societal ownership of any policy reform or ways forward that we all believe are necessary.*
> (Tandon, 1998b)

CONCLUSION

The participation of the poor in donor-funded projects and policy formulation finally has come to be accepted as an imperative of development. After 30 years of development work, beginning in 1979 and continuing for the next 15 years, development donor agencies came to the realization that poor and marginalized people needed to be integrally involved in aid projects or policies intended to benefit them. This realization, and the subsequent efforts to incorporate participation of the poor throughout these donor agencies, have begun to yield sustainable improvements in social and economic conditions of poor people. Moreover, these efforts are empowering poor people to take more active roles in the development of their locality, their region or even their country. Their capacity and that of other participants is increasing. Such involvement of the poor in major development initiatives is an expression of democratization. As many participants in the 1998 Participation Conference said, the participation of the poor is a right of citizenship – the right to be informed about and involved in the development of one's country.

Do these changes represent a paradigm shift in development thinking? Mounting evidence points in that direction. Increasingly, around the world, citizens are asserting themselves and demanding to be heard by their governments. Recipient governments in many countries are redefining their roles and engaging more with their citizens in seeking new development solutions. Within the donor institutions, changes in thinking are occurring as well. Whereas at the World Bank in the 1980s the major focus was on economic growth as the primary path to development, now the World Bank, like other donors, knows that economic growth with equity is the appropriate focus. But more than that, donors are also recognizing that citizens must be involved in a meaningful way in the policy debates and development initiatives that their governments under-take. SIDA, which adopted a participatory approach to development long before other donors, has defined participation as a basic democratic right since 1981 (Rudqvist, 1992). But for most donors, the change in view is much more recent. Andrew Norton from DFID said at the 1998 Participation Conference:

> *There is a new agenda emerging. Participation is not seen just as an option to improve effectiveness, but is seen in a new context where it is linked to governance, human rights, and strengthening accountability, policy and institutional systems… So that [government] can respond better to the needs of society and the poor and the excluded in particular.* (Norton, 1998)

USAID's paper prepared for the same conference said:

> *Perhaps more fundamentally, it is sound to remember that participation is essentially a matter of citizenship – a matter of people having access to opportunity and to the full range of their society's decision-making processes. USAID views participation not only as an essential feature of effective development work, but as a purpose of development itself.* (La Voy and Charles, 1998)

The World Bank's adoption of a joint World Bank–IMF poverty reduction strategy paper as the way borrowing countries can qualify for debt relief under the most heavily indebted poor countries is the most recent sign that it, too, recognizes the need for widespread citizen involvement. The chairman of the World Bank's board summarized a board discussion on the strategy in this way:

> *There was general agreement with the principles underlying the poverty reduction strategy papers, namely: that they should be country driven with broad participation of elected bodies, civil society and development partners; that they should reflect the country specific nature and determinants of poverty; and that they should be results oriented and link public actions to poverty outcomes, especially through faster and broad-based growth.* (World Bank, 1999b)

Rajesh Tandon had this to say at the end of the 1998 Participation Conference:

> *I believe that the new concerns of partnership, of inclusion, of accountability and transparency in governance are fundamentally rooted in the very act of citizen participation at the base. We understand why obstacles exist to their participation today. These are structural obstacles, economic and political obstacles. These are obstacles rooted in their culture and tradition. Unless we address these obstacles, we will not be able to create the foundation on which our aspirations for partnership, for inclusion and for good governance can ever be realized.* (Tandon, 1998b)

Many have been involved in these efforts to enable the poor to take their rightful place in development. Leaders and staff of donor organizations, personnel of government implementing agencies, NGOs, contractors, academics and research institutes have all played a part, and continue to do so. The job of incorporating participation in donor and recipient agencies is far from over. But it is work that is well underway and that, with continued commitment and effort, holds great promise of success.

Notes

Chapter 1 Introduction

1 Several of these workshops gave rise to special issues of *RRA* (Rapid Rural Appraisal) *Notes*, which in 1995 became *PLA* (Participatory Learning and Appraisal) *Notes*. These were published by IIED and quickly achieved a wide circulation. One workshop at IDS was the basis for *The Myth of Community: Gender Issues in Participatory Development* (Gujit and Shah, 1998), and another in 1996 gave rise to two more books, *Whose Voice? Participatory Research and Policy Change* (Holland and Blackburn, 1998b) and *Who Changes? Institutionalizing Participation in Development* (Blackburn and Holland, 1998a). IDS is now regarded as a leader in the study and promotion of participation in development

Chapter 2 The World Bank and NGOs: The Evolution of a Participation Policy

1 At the time, Dr Serageldin was Director in the World Bank's Africa Region. He later became Vice President of Environmentally and Socially Sustainable Development, the department where extensive engagement with NGOs took place, and a co-chair of the NGO–World Bank Committee in 1997–1998
2 This group had succeeded in convincing the Bank to pay more attention to poverty as part of its mission (an issue NGOs had been promoting vigorously as well). The group also had succeeded in getting the topic of military spending on the agenda of the IMF
3 This work of the NIA had had support from the Ford Foundation, which funded an 'inside/outside' advisory working group. This group was comprised of NIA bureaucrats and outside academics, and included Korten, who was Ford's regional representative at the time. This group was devised as a 'learning' group composed of individual volunteers, advisory in nature and intended only to develop improved programme methods based on experience in pilot projects: it was a 'learning strategy that would assist the NIA in transforming its communal irrigation devel-

opment program.' The premise of the group was that 'lasting change comes about through a social learning process in which many people throughout an organization gradually come to see their task and roles in new ways, often due to new and enriched feedback mechanisms' (Korten and Siy, 1988)

4   The 20 projects were chosen from approximately 80 nominated. The group tracked these projects and analysed them as to their participatory or non-participatory nature. For each nomination, both the task manager and division manager had to agree that the project be proposed for study by the Learning Group. Each project chosen was given a sum of money from a SIDA trust fund to enable the study. The Learning Group agreed on a set of 21 priority questions to use in the investigation of the 20 projects. Half the questions centred on the World Bank's capacity to support participation in activities it finances; the other half dealt with general issues related to participation in borrowing countries (Bhatnagar and Williams, 1992)

5   This 'Addendum to the Report of the Participatory Development Learning Group' was drafted by Nancy Alexander and 26 other members of the final workshop at the Participation Conference: all were from NGOs or universities and all signed the cover letter, although not all made comments

6   IDA-1O replenishment means the tenth time that the IDA's funding has been replenished

7   An example of this was the February 1992 workshop. In preparation, seven papers were commissioned by the World Bank from academics, NGOs, and bilateral and multilateral donor representatives regarding aspects of participation or their agencies' experiences in participation. These papers, in addition to three prepared by World Bank staff, were provided to all workshop participants as well as the 21 questions the Learning Group was using to study participation. With the papers as resource material, the questions were discussed in detail in small groups, with recommendations emanating from these discussions

8   Picciotto has written three papers on participation. See *Participatory Development: Myths and Dilemmas*, World Bank, 1992; *Putting Institutional Economics to Work: From Participation to Governance*, World Bank, 1995; and with Neelima Grover, 'Rural Development: Hierarchy or Participation', 1996

9   A sum of US$2 million was allocated in financial year 1995, US$1.5 million in 1996 and US$ 750,000 in 1997 (pers com)

10   This project was designed to address poverty in Western China. It involved the resettlement of some 58,000 people from eastern Qinghai Province to Dulan County in the west, and would have supported the creation of a water storage dam, large-scale irrigation, and the transformation of an arid ecosystem populated by Tibetan and Mongolian nomadic herders to an agricultural oasis. When the project came to light during April 1999, Tibetans in Dulan County smuggled letters out to Tibetan exiles in the West that requested help to stop the project, which

they believed threatened their cultural survival. Tibetans form 25 per cent of the population in this region, a number that would be dwarfed by the groups moving in. Their concerns and those raised by an international network of Tibet support groups and human rights organizations were echoed by environmental groups who questioned the sustainability of the project (Treakle, 2000)

11 The Institute is a nonprofit organization that seeks to inform, nurture and motivate concerned citizens for action on policies that affect hungry people (Bread for the World Institute, Development Bank Watchers' Project, 1998)

12 An illustration of the hard-line approach is the way in which the World Bank came to agree to undertake SAPRI. In 1993 the '50 Years Is Enough' campaign was launched by six NGOs. Soon 200 NGOs around the world joined the effort. The purpose of the campaign was to call attention to the World Bank's real record, to call for an end to the imposition of its economic prescriptions on borrower governments, and to encourage more open, democratic response to local priorities in these countries. In the absence of these changes, the campaign called for reduced funding and influence for the World Bank. The campaign focused on providing the media with information that countered the World Bank's own information. The media responded more enthusiastically than expected, and many influential newspapers and magazines carried critical stories of the organization, with a negative impact on its public image. When James Wolfensohn became World Bank president in June 1995, he was particularly sensitive to the '50 Years' campaign. In the view of many involved with SAPRI, he accepted the SAPRI proposal for two reasons. He wanted to broaden the thinking of World Bank staff and recognized the importance of engagement with civil society and other participants in development in doing so; and he also understood the public relations necessity of making an effort to engage in dialogue with civil society regarding economic policies (pers com, 25 July 2000)

Chapter 4 Incorporating Participation of the Poor in International Development Agencies

1 Much has been written about efforts to adapt organization change theory to public institutions. See *The Empowered Manager: Positive political skills at work* (Block, 1986); *Seamless Government: A practical guide to re-engineering in the public sector* (Linden, 1994); and *Managing Chaos and Complexity in Government: A new paradigm for managing change, innovation and organizational renewal* (Kiel, 1994)

2 A sum of US$2 million was allocated in 1995, US$1.5 million in 1996 and US$ 750,000 in 1997 (pers com, 7 Jun 2000)

Chapter 6   Lessons Learned and Implications for Participation of the Poor

1   The International Bank for Reconstruction and Development (IBRD) is one of five agencies that comprise the World Bank Group. The others are the International Development Association (IDA), the International Finance Corporation (IFC), the Multilateral Investment Guarantee Agency (MIGA) and the International Centre for Settlement of Investment Disputes (ICSID). Each is legally and financially distinct from the others. The IBRD and the IDA share the same staff and facilities. The IBRD works primarily with middle-income countries, and the IDA with the poorest countries. The IBRD and IDA have three related functions: to lend money; to provide economic advice and technical assistance; and to serve as a catalyst to investment by others. The IFC works directly with the private sector in recipient countries, and MICA encourages direct foreign investment in member countries by protecting investors from non-commercial risk. The ICISD provided for conciliation and the arbitration of disputes between member countries and investors who qualify as nationals of other countries. Over the years, the vast majority of NGO advocacy has been carried out toward the IBRD and the IDA, although in recent years, NGOs have begun work to convince the Bank to 'harmonize' IBRD and IDA policies with the IFC and MIGA that relate to such topics as information disclosure, environment and participation.

References

ActionAid Kenya (1998) 'Monitoring Participation in World Bank Programs', report for NGOWG, July

African Charter for Popular Participation in Development and Transformation (1990) written and adopted at *International Conference on Popular Participation*, February, Arusha, Tanzania

Alexander, N *et al* (1994) 'Addendum to the Report of the Participatory Development Learning Group' in *The World Bank and Participation*, World Bank, Operations Policy Department, Annex VI, Washington, DC

Arruda, M (1993) Memorandum to NGOWG Members Ref: Brief History of the NGOWG, 25 July, Geneva

Atwood, J B (1993) 'Statement of Principles on Participatory Development', meeting presentation, November, USAID, Washington, DC

Aycrigg, M (1998) 'Participation and the World Bank: Successes, Constraints, and Responses', Social Development Papers 29, The World Bank, Washington, DC

Baima de Borri, M, Palomares, M and Scavuzzo, J A (1998) *Second Report on Rural Initiative and Poverty Relief Program Monitoring PROINDER*, summary, Córdoba, Argentina

Bamberger, M (1998) *The Role of Community Participation in Development Planning and Project Management*, World Bank, Economic Development Institute, Washington, DC

Bank Information Center (BIC) (1999) *BIC's Comments on the Draft 'World Bank Policy on Information Disclosure Issues Paper'*, 15 December, Washington, DC

Bhatnagar, B and Williams, A C (eds) (1992) *Participatory Development and the World Bank*, World Bank Discussion Papers 183, World Bank, Washington, DC

Blackburn, J and de Toma, C (1998) 'Scaling-down as the Key to Scaling Up? The Role of Participatory Municipal Planning in Bolivia's Law of Popular Participation' in Blackburn, J and Holland, J (eds) *Who Changes? Institutionalizing Participation in Development*, Intermediate Technology Publications, London

Blackburn, J and Holland, J (eds) (1998) *Who Changes? Institutionalizing Participation in Development*, Intermediate Technology Publications, London

Block, P (1986) *The Empowered Manager: Positive Political Skills at Work,* Jossey-Bass Inc, San Francisco

Blustein, P (1996) 'Missionary work', *The Washington Post Magazine,* 10 November

Boyle, N (1998) *Putting Theory and Practice to Work in Institutional Development (ID): A Case Study and Analysis,* World Bank, Washington, DC

Bread for the World Institute (1998) *Who Shapes Your Country's Future? A guide to influencing the World Bank's Country Assistance Strategies,* Bread for the World Institute, Silver Spring, MD (not published)

Brown, L D and Tandon, R (1983) 'Ideology and political economy in inquiry: Action Research and Participatory Research', *The Journal of Applied Behavioral Science,* vol 19, no 3, pp278–279

Bruns, B and Soelaiman, I (undated) *From Policy to Practice: Agency and NGO in Indonesia's Program to Turn Small Irrigation Systems Over to Farmers ,* Institute for Social and Economic Research, Education and Information (LP3ES), Jakarta, Indonesia (not published)

Canadian International Development Agency (CIDA) (1997) *Mainstreaming Participatory Development: Experiences and Lessons of the Inter-Agency Group on Participation,* CIDA, Ottawa, Ontario, Canada

Carduner, O (1996) *Reengineering at USAID/Bolivia: Why We Did What We Did,* paper prepared for USAID, Bolivia

Cernea, M M (1985) *Putting People First: Sociological Variables in Rural Development,* Oxford University Press, Oxford

Chambers, R (1997) *Whose Reality Counts? Putting the First Last,* Intermediate Technology Publications, London

Chambers, R (1998) 'Foreword' in Holland, J with Blackburn, J (eds) *Whose Voice? Participatory Research and Policy Change,* Intermediate Technology Publications, London

Chambers, R and Blackburn, J (1996) *The Power of Participation: PRA and Policy,* IDS Policy Briefing, no 7, IDS, Brighton

Chiriboga, M (1999) 'Constructing a Southern Constituency for Global Advocacy: The Experience of Latin American NGOs and the World Bank', paper presented at conference *NGOs in the Global Future,* 11–13 January, University of Birmingham, UK

Clark, J and Dorschel, W (1998) *Civil Society Participation in World Bank Country Assistance Strategies – Lessons from Experience, FY 97–98,* World Bank, Washington, DC

Covey, J C (1998) 'Is Critical Cooperation Possible? Influencing the World Bank through Operational Collaboration and Policy Dialogue', in Fox, J A and Brown, L D (eds) *The Struggle for Accountability: The World Bank, NGOs, and Grassroots Movements,* MIT Press, Cambridge, MA

Davis, G (1998) 'World Bank Mainstreaming Results', paper presented at conference *Upscaling and Mainstreaming Participation of Primary Stakeholders: Lessons Learned and Ways Forward,* World Bank, Washington, DC

Dollar, D and Pritchett, L (1998) *Assessing Aid: What works, what doesn't and why,* Oxford University Press for the World Bank, New York

EcoNews, Kenya, (1998) 'Sexually Transmitted Infections, Kenya: Summary of Monitoring Case Study for NGOWG', EcoNews, Nairobi, Kenya

Edwards, M and Hulme, D (eds) (1995) *Non-Governmental Organizations: Performance and Accountability,* Earthscan, London

Feeney, P (1998) *Accountable Aid: Local Participation in Major Projects,* Oxfam GB, Oxford

Finsterbusch, K and Van Wicklin W (1987) 'The Contribution of Beneficiary Participation to Development Project Effectiveness', *Public Administration and Development,* vol 7, no 1, pp1–23

Forster, R (1998a) 'GTZ's experience with Mainstreaming Primary Stakeholder Participation', paper presented at conference *Upscaling and Mainstreaming Participation of Primary Stakeholders: Lessons Learned and Ways Forward,* World Bank, Washington, DC

Forster, R (1998b) Presentation of GTZ report at conference *Upscaling and Mainstreaming participation of Primary Stakeholders: Lessons Learned and Ways Forward,* 19–20 November, transcript

Fox, J A and Brown, D L (eds) (1998) *The Struggle for Accountability: The World Bank, NGOs and Grassroots Movements,* MIT Press, Cambridge, MA

Freedman, J (1998) 'Simplicities and Complexities of Participatory Evaluation' in Jackson, E T and Kassam, Y (eds) *Knowledge Shared: Participatory Evaluation in Development Cooperation,* Kumarian Press, West Hartford, CT

Freire, P (1974) *Pedagogy of the Oppressed,* Seabury Press, New York

Gray, A (1998) ' Development Policy, Development Protest: The World Bank, Indigenous Peoples, and NGOs' in Fox, J A and Brown, L D (eds) *The Struggle for Accountability: The World Bank, NGOs and Grassroots Movements,* MIT Press, Cambridge, MA

Group Six (1998) 'Institutional Reforms and Renewal', Mini-Workshop Report at conference *Upscaling and Mainstreaming Participation of Primary Stakeholders: Lessons Learned and Ways Forward,* World Bank, Washington, DC

Group Three (1998) 'Capacity Building of Primary Stakeholders', Mini-Workshop Report at conference *Upscaling and Mainstreaming Participation of Primary Stakeholders: Lessons Learned and Ways Forward,* World Bank, Washington, DC

Group Three-A (1998) 'Enabling Government Implementing Agencies to Mainstream Participation', Mini-Workshop Report at conference *Upscaling and Mainstreaming Participation of Primary Stakeholders: Lessons Learned and Ways Forward,* World Bank, Washington, DC

Guijt, Irene and Shah, Meera (eds) (1998) *The Myth of Community: Gender Issues in Participatory Development,* Intermediate Technology Publications, London

Haas, E B (1990) *When Knowledge Is Power,* University of California Press, Berkeley

Hagmann, J, Chuma, E and Murwira, K (1998) 'Scaling-up of Participatory Approaches through Institutionalization in Government Services: The Case of Agricultural Extension in Masvingo Province, Zimbabwe' in Blackburn, J and Holland, J (eds) *Who Changes? Institutionalizing Participation in Development,* Intermediate Technology Publications, London

Hellinger, S (2000) pers com, 27 July, Washington, DC

Holland, J and Blackburn, J (eds) (1998a) *Who Changes? Institutionalizing Participation in Development,* Intermediate Technology Publications, London

Holland, J and Blackburn, J (eds) (1998b) *Whose Voice? Participatory Research and Policy Change,* Intermediate Technology Publications, London

INADES-Formation (1998) *The Community-Based Natural Resource and Wildlife Management (GEPRENAF) Project, Côte d'Ivoire,* Case Study Summary

InterAction (1992) 'Memorandum from Carolyn Long to Aubrey Williams regarding the mid-term report of the learning group on participation', Washington, DC

InterAction, (1999) *Assessment of Participatory Approaches in Identification of World Bank Projects,* InterAction, Washington, DC

INTRAC (1998) *The Participatory Approaches Learning Study (PALS): Executive Summary and Recommendations,* UK Department for International Development, Social Development Division, London

Jackson, E T (1998) 'Indicators of Change: Results-based Management and Participatory Evaluation', in Jackson, E T and Kassam Y (eds) *Knowledge Shared: Participatory Evaluation in Development Cooperation,* Kumarian Press, West Hartford, CT

Keck, M E and Sikkink, C (1998) *Beyond Borders,* Cornell University Press, Ithaca, NY

Kiel, L D (1994) *Managing Chaos and Complexity in Government: a New Paradigm for Managing Change, Innovation and Organizational Renewal,* Jossey-Bass, San Francisco

Korten, F F and Siy, Jr, R Y (1988) *Transforming a Bureaucracy: The Experience of the Philippine National Irrigation Administration,* Kumarian Press, West Hartford, CT

La Voy, D and Charles, C (1998) *Engaging 'Customer' Participation: USAID's Organizational Change Experience,* Washington DC

Linden, R M (1994) *Seamless Government: A Practical Guide to Re-engineering in the Public Sector,* Jossey-Bass, San Francisco

Long, C (1992) Personal notes

Narayan, D, Chambers, R, Shah, M K and Petesch, P (2000) *Voices of the Poor: Crying Out for Change,* OUP for the World Bank, New York

Narayan, D and Kochar, R (undated) 'ENVSP Review of Local and Community Driven Development Projects', *Environment Department Dissemination Notes no 58,* World Bank, Social Policy and Resettlement Division, Environment Department, Washington, DC

Narayan, D, Isham, J and Pritchett, L (1995) *The Contribution of People's Participation: Evidence from 121 Rural Water Supply Projects*, Environmentally Sustainable Development Occasional Paper no 1, World Bank, Washington, DC

NGOWG (1991) *The Saly Declaration*, paper written at NGO–World Bank Steering Committee meeting, March, Saly, Senegal

NGOWG (1996) Minutes of Second Latin America and Caribbean Regional Meeting, Managua, Nicaragua

NGOWG (1998) Minutes of Fourth Asia Pacific Regional Meeting, Bangkok, Thailand

Norton, A (1998) Presentation of DFID's experience in participation at conference *Upscaling and Mainstreaming Participation of Primary Stakeholders: Lessons Learned and Ways Forward*, World Bank, Washington, DC

Nyoni, S (1992) 'Keynote Address' at InterAction Forum, *Monday Developments*, 27–29 April 1992, Arlington, VA

OECD/DAC (1996) *Shaping the 21st Century: The Contribution of Development Cooperation*, Paris

Participation Sub-Group (1998) 'Upscaling and Mainstreaming Participation of Primary Stakeholders', design paper in preparation for November Participation Conference, NGOWG, New Delhi

Paul, S (1987) *Community Participation in Development Projects: The World Bank experience*, World Bank, Washington, DC

Peters, T J and Waterman R H Jr, (1982) *In Search of Excellence: Lessons from America's Best-run Companies*, Harper & Row, New York

Philippines Rural Reconstruction Movement (1998) *The Second Rural Communal Irrigation Development Project (CIDP-II)*, *Philippines*, Case Study Summary, report prepared for NGOWG, Manila, Philippines (not published)

Picciotto, R (1992) *Participatory Development: Myths and Dilemmas*, World Bank, Washington, DC

Picciotto, R (1995) *Putting Institutional Economics to Work: from Participation to Governance*, World Bank, Washington, DC

Picciotto, R and Grover, N (1996) 'Rural Development: Hierarchy or Participation', paper presented to the Annual Conference of the Southern Economic Association, Washington, DC

Pratt, B (1998) 'The Participatory Approaches Learning Study (PALS)' INTRAC's report presented at conference *Upscaling and Mainstreaming Participation of Primary Stakeholders: Lessons Learned and Ways Forward*, World Bank, Washington, DC

Pratt, B (2000), personal communication

Rietbergen-McCracken, J and Narayan, D (1998) *Participation and Social Assessment, Tools and Techniques*, World Bank, Washington, DC

Robb, C (1998) 'PPAs: A Review of the World Bank's Experience', in Holland, J and Blackburn, J (eds) *Whose Voice? Participatory Research and Policy Change*, Intermediate Technology Publications, London

Rudqvist, A (1992) 'The Swedish International Development Authority: Experience with Popular Participation', in Bhatnagar, B and Williams, A C (eds) (1992) *Participatory Development and the World Bank*, World Bank Discussion Papers no 183, Washington, DC

Salmen, L (1987) *Listen to the People*, Oxford University Press, New York

Samarthan-Centre for Development Support (1998) *Monitoring Participation in the District Primary Education Programme in Madhya Pradesh*, Bhopal, prepared for NGOWG (not published)

SEHAS (1998) *Rural Initiatives and Poverty Relief (PROINDER), Argentina*, Case Study Summary, report prepared for NGOWG, Córdoba, Argentina

Senge, P M (1990) *The Fifth Discipline: The Art and Practice of the Learning Organization*, Doubleday/Currency, New York

Shah, P and Tikare, S (1999) 'Participation in the CAS Retrospective, FY 00', World Bank, Washington, DC

Shepherd, A (1998) 'Participatory Environmental Management: Contradiction of Process, Project and Bureaucracy in the Himalayan Foothills', in Blackburn, J and Holland, J (eds) *Who Changes? Institutionalizing Participation in Development*, Intermediate Technology Publications, London

Tandon, R (1995) NGO Working Group – Sub-Group memorandum on Participation, prepared for NGOWG

Tandon, R (1996a) 'Participation and the World Bank: Primary Lessons', report presented at NGO–World Bank Committee meeting in October in Washington, DC, Society for Participatory Research in Asia (PRIA), New Delhi

Tandon, R (1996b) 'Strengthening Participation of Primary Stakeholders: An Action Plan for the NGO Working Group', paper presented at NGO–World Bank Committee meeting in Washington, DC, Society for Participatory Research in Asia (PRIA), New Delhi

Tandon, R (1998a) Results of Monitoring World Bank Projects, presentation at conference *Upscaling and Mainstreaming Participation of Primary Stakeholders: Lessons Learned and Ways Forward*, World Bank, Washington, DC

Tandon, R (1998b) Presentation at conference *Upscaling and Mainstreaming Participation of Primary Stakeholders: Lessons Learned and Ways Forward*, World Bank, Washington, DC

Tandon, R and Cordeiro, A (1998) *Participation of Primary Stakeholders in World Bank's Project and Policy Work*, Society for Participatory Research in Asia (PRIA), New Delhi

Tendler, J (1997) *Good Government in the Tropics*, Johns Hopkins University Press, Baltimore

Thompson, J (1995) 'Participatory Approaches in Government Bureaucracies: Facilitating the Process of Institutional Change', *World Development*, vol 23, no 9, pp1521–1554

Thompson, J (1998) 'Participatory Social Assessment in an Economy in Transition: Strengthening Capacity and Influencing Policy in Estonia' in

Blackburn, J and Holland, J (eds) *Who Changes? Institutionalizing Participation in Development*, Intermediate Technology Publications, London

Udall, L 'The World Bank and Public Accountability: Has Anything Changed?' in Fox, J A and Brown, L D (eds) (1998) *The Struggle for Accountability: The World Bank, NGOs and Grassroots Movements*, MIT Press, Cambridge, MA

United Nations (1993) *Human Development Report 1993*, Oxford University Press, New York

United Nations (1997) *Human Development Report 1997*, Oxford University Press, New York

United Nations (1999) *Human Development Report 1999*, Oxford University Press, New York

USAID (1995) glossary definition, Automated Directives Service (ADS) no 201, Washington, DC: USAID

USAID (1999) *Reform Roadmap, 1999–2000*, USAID, Washington, DC

Van Wicklin, W (1998) 'Design Paper, OED Participation Process Review', World Bank Operations Evaluation Department, Washington, DC (not published)

Webster's Encyclopedic Unabridged Dictionary of the English Language (1996) Portland House, New York

Williams, A C (1998) personal communication

Williams, A C (1998) 'Reflections on the World Bank's Learning Group on Participation', World Bank, Washington, DC

Williams, L (1997) (ed) *Gender Equity and the World Bank Group: A Post-Beijing Assessment*, Women's Eyes on the World Bank–US in collaboration with Women's Eyes on the World Bank–Latin America, 50 Years Is Enough, and US Network for Global Economic Justice, Washington, DC

Wolfensohn, J D (1997) 'The Challenge of Inclusion', address to the Board of Governors, World Bank Group, Hong Kong

Wolfensohn, J D (1998) Presentation at conference *Upscaling and Mainstreaming Participation of Primary Stakeholders: Lessons Learned and Ways Forward*, World Bank, Washington, DC

Wolfensohn, J D (1999) *A Proposal for a Comprehensive Development Framework: A discussion draft*, World Bank, Washington, DC

World Bank (1992) *Report of the Portfolio Management Task Force*, World Bank, Washington, DC

World Bank (1993) *Getting Results: The World Bank's Agenda for Improving Development Effectiveness*, World Bank, Washington, DC

World Bank (1994a) *Fund for Innovative Approaches in Human and Social Development*, World Bank, Washington, DC

World Bank (1994b) *The World Bank and Participation*, The World Bank, Operations Policy Department, Washington, DC

World Bank (1996a) *The World Bank Participation Sourcebook*, World Bank, Washington, DC

World Bank (1996b) *The World Bank's Partnership with Nongovernmental Organizations*, World Bank, Poverty and Social Policy Department, Washington, DC

World Bank (1997a) *IDA in Action 1993–1996: The Pursuit of Sustained Poverty Reduction, Summary*, World Bank, Washington, DC

World Bank (1997b) *Renewal at the World Bank: Working Better for a Better World*, World Bank, Washington, DC

World Bank (1997c) *World Development Report: The State in a Changing World*, World Bank, Washington, DC

World Bank (1998) *Renewal at the World Bank: One-year progress report*, World Bank, Washington, DC

World Bank (1999a) *Building Poverty Reduction Strategies in Developing Countries*, Poverty Reduction and Economic Management, World Bank Group, Washington, DC

World Bank (1999b) 'Poverty Reduction Strategy Papers: Operational Issues', memo, World Bank, Washington, DC

World Bank (1999c) *Conclusions of the Board's Second Review of the Inspection Panel*, World Bank, Washington, DC

Index